ETHAN EXPOSED

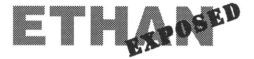

Also by Eric Orner

The Mostly Unfabulous Social Life of Ethan Green

The Seven Deadly Sins of Love

The Ethan Green Chronicles

Illustrated by Eric Orner

Husband Hunting Made Easy by Patrick Price

Eric Orner

St. Martin's Griffin
New York

Front and back cover design by Judy Dombrowski

ISBN 0-312-20040-4

First St. Martin's Griffin Edition: August 1999

10 9 8 7 6 5 4 3 2 1

For Steve......

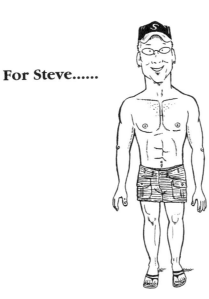

And, as always, enormous thanks to Ardys Kozbial for invaluable editing, proofing, and idea bouncing. And to my editor at St. Martin's Press, Keith Kahla, for making this book possible . . .

Introduction

When I finish reading another installment of Eric Orner's *Mostly Unfabulous Social Life of Ethan Green,* my laughter and admiration often give way to a twinge of discontent. There are times when I want Life itself to be more like a cartoon. The advantages are readily apparent to the readers of Ethan Green.

In Ethan's world painful situations like rejection, infidelity, breaking up with a boyfriend, thankless jobs, awkward dinner parties, being single on Valentine's Day, having your cat misbehave at the veterinarian's office, and even appearing on television with a noticeable hair growing out of the top of your ear are presented with a perfect mixture of detailed observation, hilarious humor, and sympathy that leaves the reader feeling exhilarated instead of depressed. In Ethan's world we're able to read other people's thoughts; the motivations and inexplicable behavior of friends, family, pets, and acquaintances are clearly captioned. In Ethan's world important details are never overlooked because directional arrows clearly point them out. In Ethan's world there are no ugly people because even the most grotesque characters are beautifully drawn.

Reading Ethan Green, every gay man, no matter how fabulous or unfabulous he may be—fabulosity being a statistic that can be hard to gauge, since the scales are notoriously unreliable—will recognize himself or, better yet, someone he knows.

Two strips in Eric Orner's latest collection are entitled *The Gay Man's Guide to All Your Relationships,* and in many ways it would be the perfect subtitle for all of Eric's work. What makes Ethan Green stand out is Eric's sharp eye for the absurdities and contradictions of human behavior as evidenced by the life and desires of one gay man. Ethan wants a boyfriend, but he also yearns for that cute boy he spotted walking down the street. He loves his biological family, but visiting them at

Thanksgiving only makes him feel thankful that he doesn't spend more time with them. He's proud to be gay, but he's rightfully embarrassed that he once demonstrated his pride by wearing a pair of rainbow suspenders.

What makes the world of Ethan so universal is its brilliant specificity. The clothing, possessions, even the tattoos of every character in Ethan's world are depicted with novelistic detail. The fruit on a kitchen table isn't held in just any bowl, it's displayed in one of those now pricey yellow mixing bowls that are the pride of antique shops around the country. And a flippant remark about a character's bizarre personal mannerism is delivered with the same intimacy as a conversation between two good friends. For instance, when Ethan takes a job working as a personal assistant for the big old queen TV weatherman Monty Poole, a "check this out" balloon in one panel indicates "Her Frank Lloyd Wright look," with Monty shown wearing one of the Taliesin master's silly-looking black hats.

One of the things that I especially admire about Eric's work is the frequent witty asides that are funny enough to have been used as the main subject of a panel. For example, an arrow will indicate a book, *Bob and Rod's Guide to Splitsville,* lying on the floor of Ethan's apartment—a title that allows the reader to conjure up a beefcake photographic tome of the two hunks dividing up their possessions in the desert, the forest, and the seashore, the three primary ecosystems of male nudity.

Eric Orner has managed a rare thing in humor. He's consistently funny and sharp, and yet he's never cynical. All of his characters—even Ethan's arch-nemesis, the unbearable Todd—are rendered lovingly, and the results are a delight.

Bob Smith
Los Angeles
March 1999

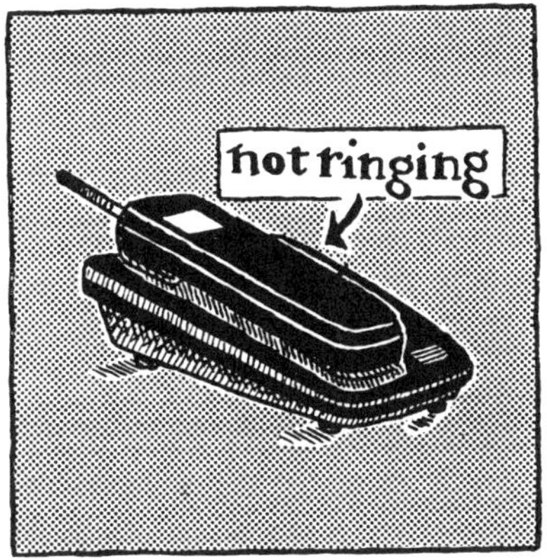
not ringing

***W**elcome to the mostly unfabulous social life of Ethan Green, where dates are scarce, cats are cynical, and "ex" boyfriends just get better-looking . . .*

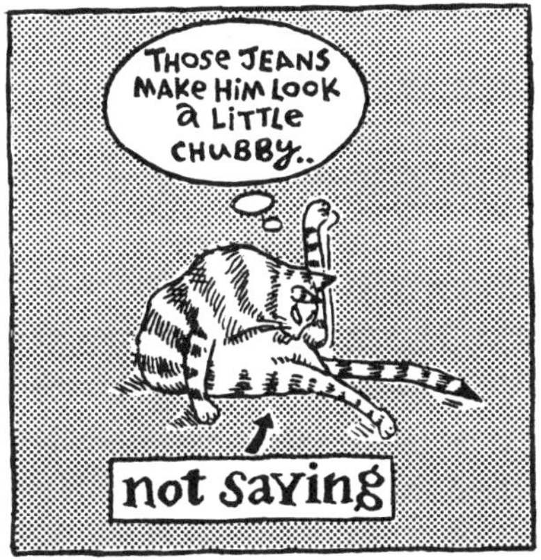
THOSE JEANS MAKE HIM LOOK A LITTLE CHUBBY..
not saying

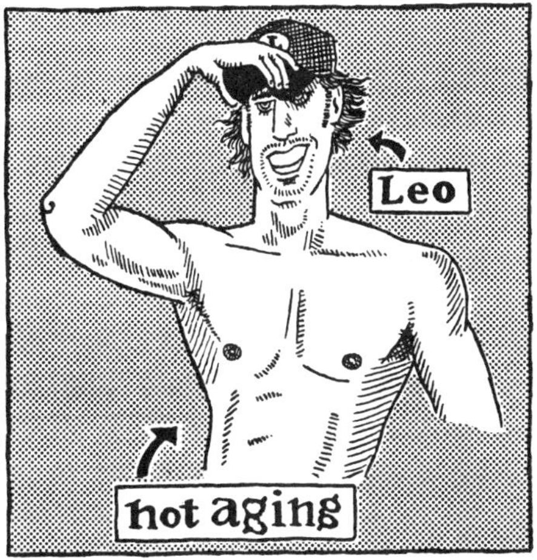
Leo
hot aging

*E*than is the hero of these stories. He's your Joe Average gay guy, doing his best to cope with life, lovers, pets, employers, and love handles . . .

2

*C*harlotte is his cool dyke neighbor. She makes the nastiest lentil soup in these United States.

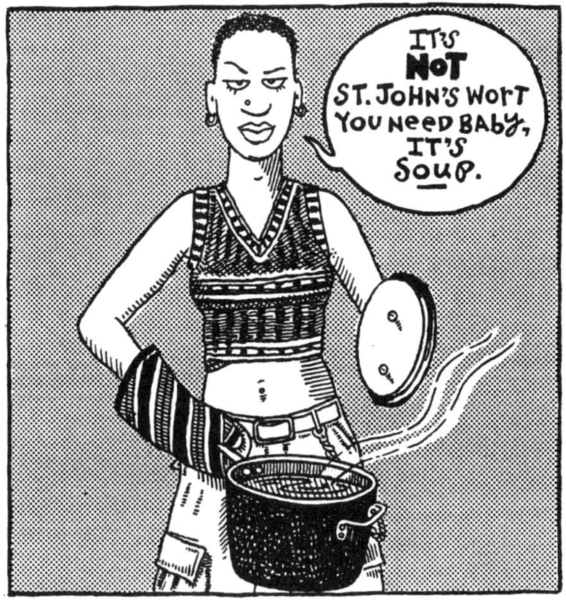
IT'S NOT ST. JOHN'S WORT YOU NEED BABY, IT'S SOUP.

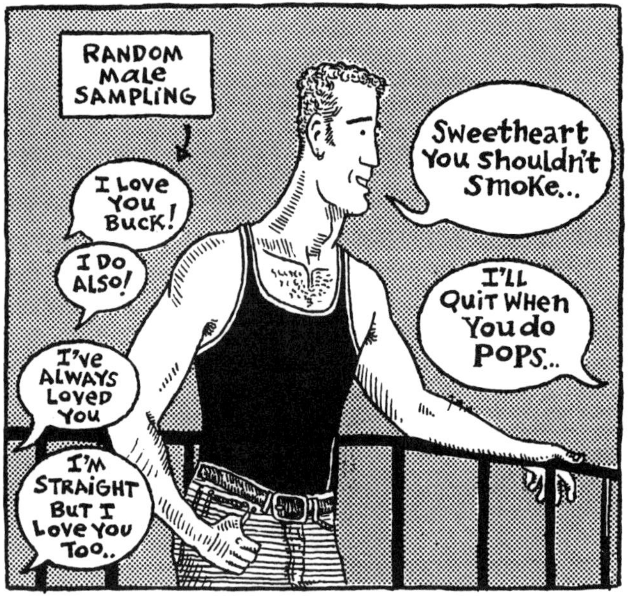
RANDOM MALE SAMPLING
I LOVE YOU BUCK!
I DO ALSO!
I'VE ALWAYS LOVED YOU
I'M STRAIGHT BUT I LOVE YOU TOO..
SWEETHEART YOU SHOULDN'T SMOKE...
I'LL QUIT WHEN YOU DO POPS..

***B**ucky is his best friend, and the object of the affections of most of the men in town . . .*

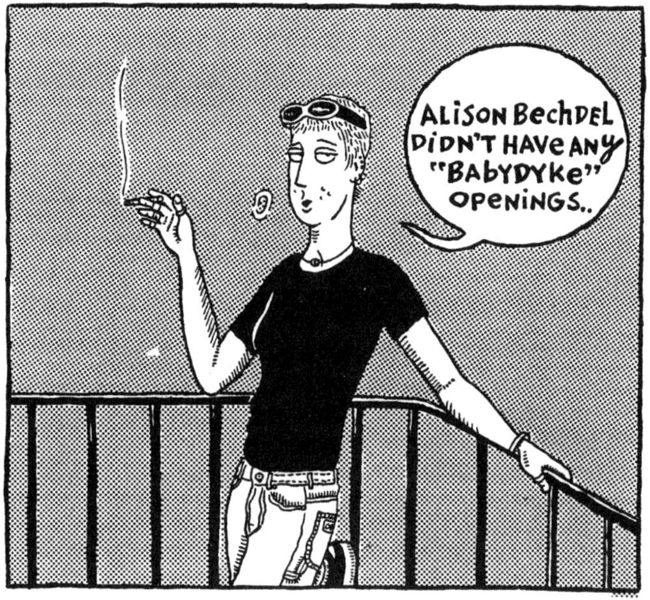
ALISON BECHDEL DIDN'T HAVE ANY "BABYDYKE" OPENINGS..

***B**uck's also the foster dad of Moon, a teenage runaway who wonders how she stumbled into this family of low-rent comic strip characters . . .*

***T*he Hat Sisters are Ethan's glamorous super-diva aunties. They're called upon regularly to remind him *not* to take it all so seriously . . .**

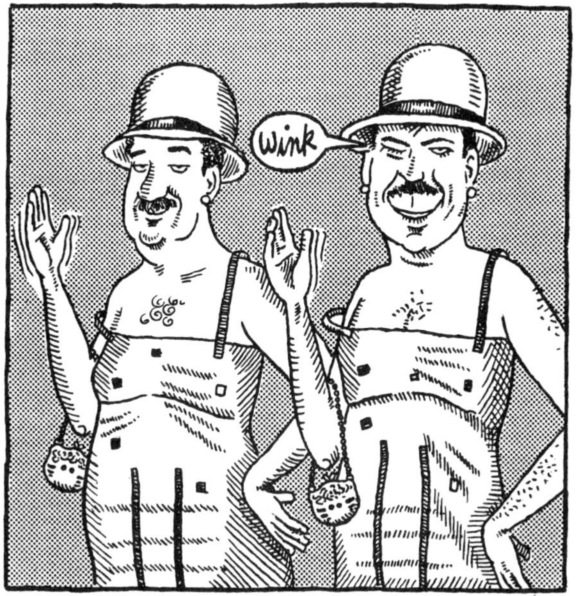
wink

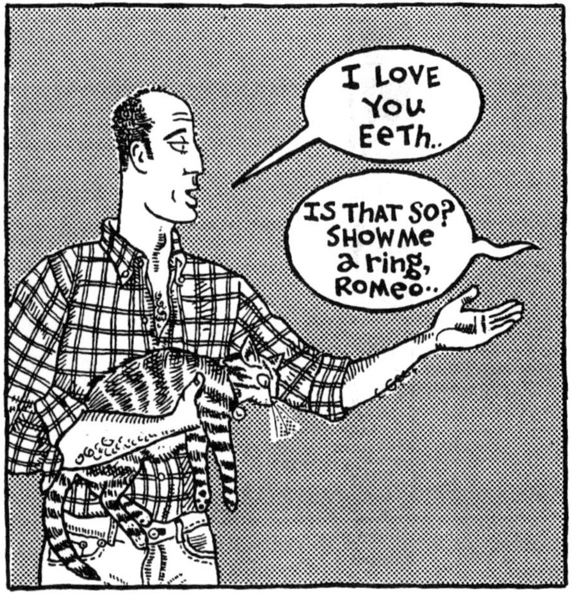
I LOVE YOU EETh..
IS THAT SO? SHOW ME a ring, ROMEO..

Doug is Eeth's on-again off-again boyfriend, who is as commitment-shy as he is hunky and sweet-natured . . .

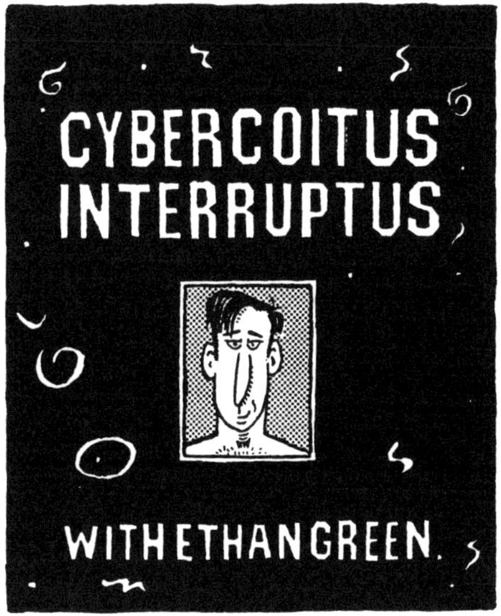
CYBERCOITUS INTERRUPTUS
WITHETHANGREEN.

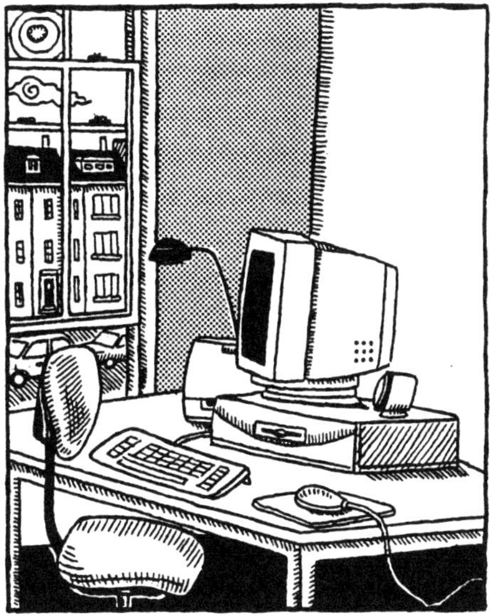

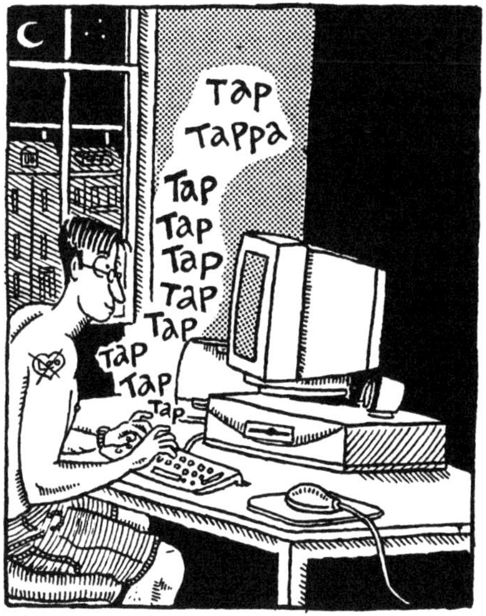
Tap
Tappa
Tap
Tap
Tap
Tap
Tap
Tap
Tap
Tap

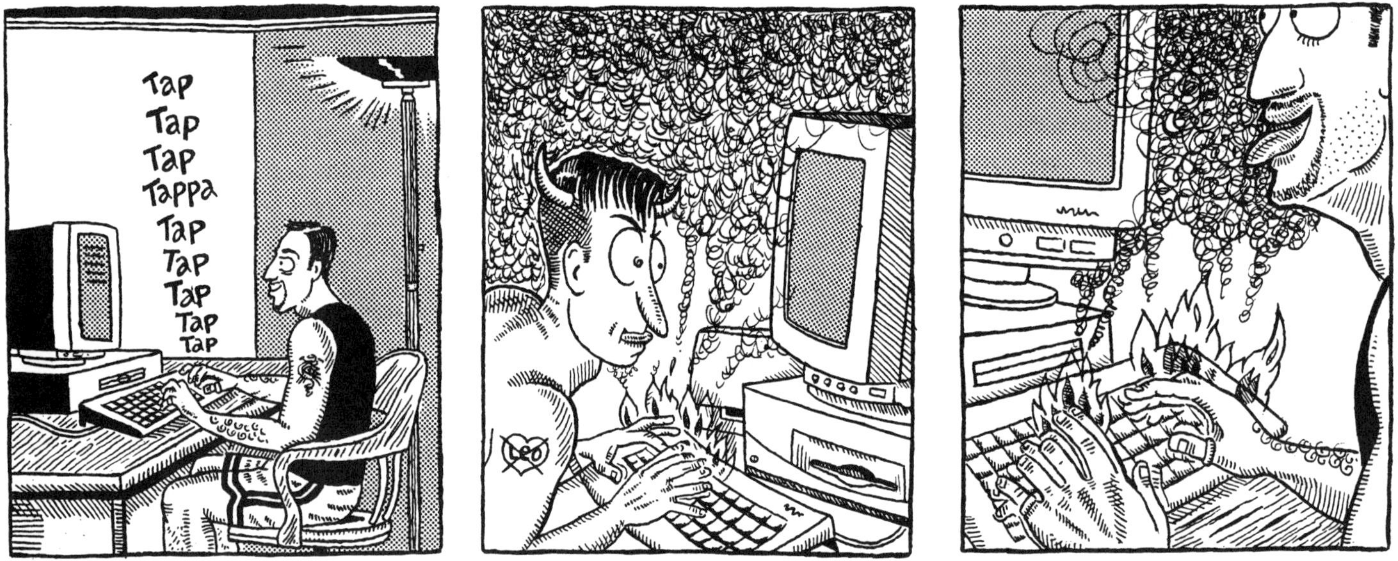
Tap
Tap
Tap
Tappa
Tap
Tap
Tap
Tap
Tap
Leo

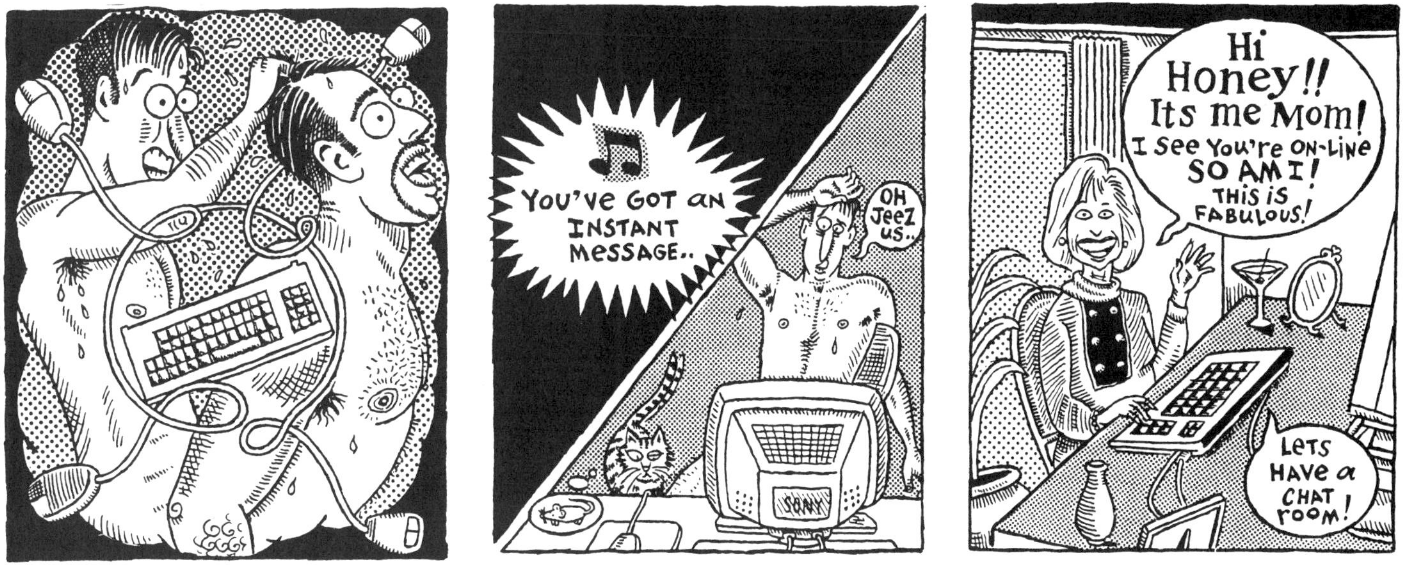
YOU'VE GOT an INSTANT MESSAGE..
OH JeeZ us..
SONY
Hi Honey!! Its me Mom! I See You're ON-LINE SO AM I! THIS iS FABULOUS!
LeTS HAVe a CHAT room!

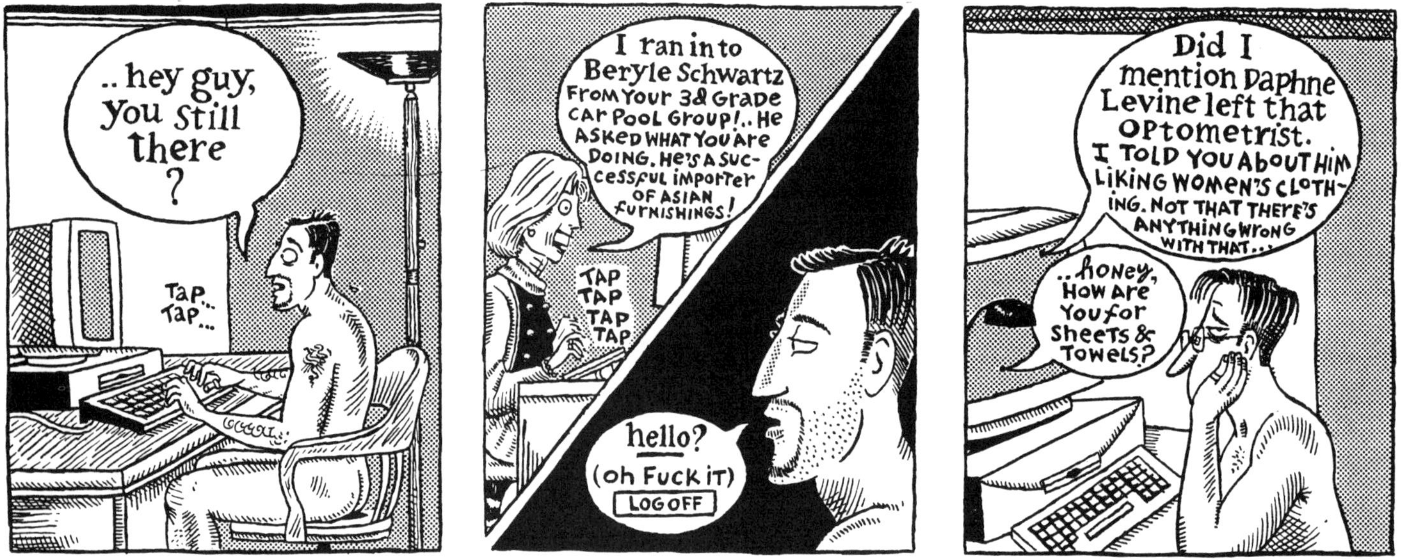
..hey guy, you still there ?
TAP... TAP...
I ran into Beryle Schwartz FROM YOUR 3d GRADE CAR POOL GROUP!.. HE ASKED WHAT YOU ARE DOING. HE'S A SUCCESSFUL IMPORTER OF ASIAN FURNISHINGS!
TAP TAP TAP TAP
hello? (oh FUCK IT) LOG OFF
Did I mention Daphne Levine left that optometrist. I TOLD YOU ABOUT HIM LIKING WOMEN'S CLOTHING. NOT THAT THERE'S ANYTHING WRONG WITH THAT...
..honey, HOW ARE YOU FOR SHEETS & TOWELS?

ethan & doug
in
Take Two
?
ONE DAY RECENTLY YOUR PHONE RINGS. IT'S YOUR "EX", DOUG.
HE ASKS YOU TO MEET HIM FOR COFFEE.
I WAS ABOUT TO GET TOGETHER WITH A COUPLE OF FRIENDS, BUT I CAN RE-SCHEDULE.
(art film)

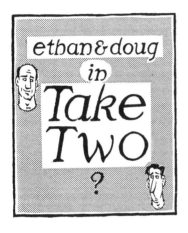

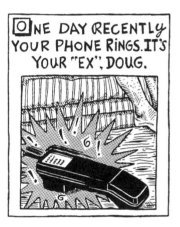

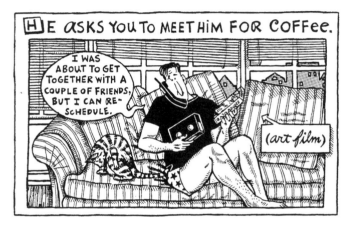

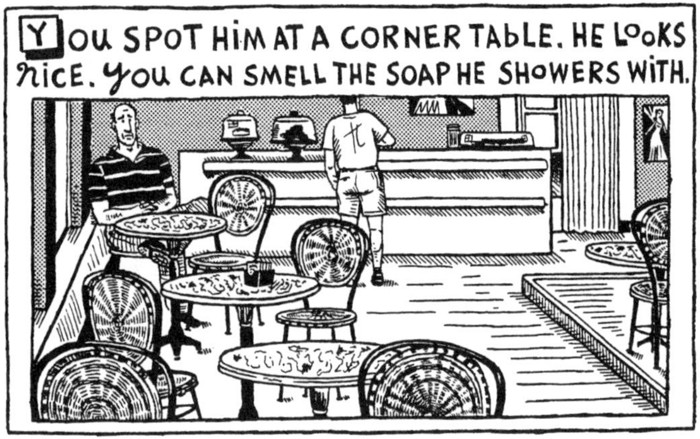
YOU SPOT HIM AT A CORNER TABLE. HE LOOKS NICE. YOU CAN SMELL THE SOAP HE SHOWERS WITH.

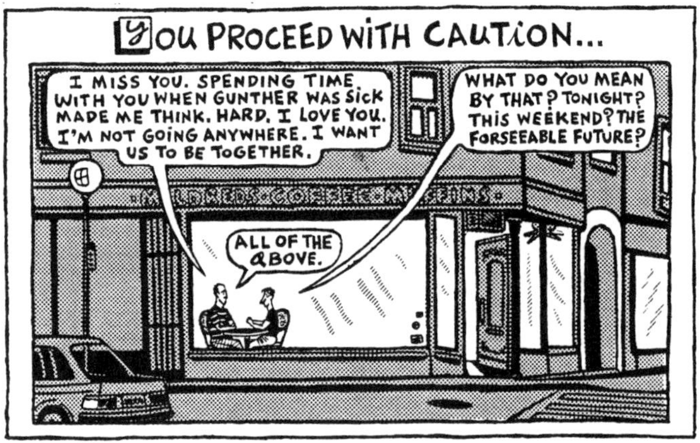
YOU PROCEED WITH CAUTION...
I MISS YOU. SPENDING TIME WITH YOU WHEN GUNTHER WAS SICK MADE ME THINK. HARD. I LOVE YOU. I'M NOT GOING ANYWHERE. I WANT US TO BE TOGETHER.
WHAT DO YOU MEAN BY THAT? TONIGHT? THIS WEEKEND? THE FORSEEABLE FUTURE?
ALL OF THE ABOVE.

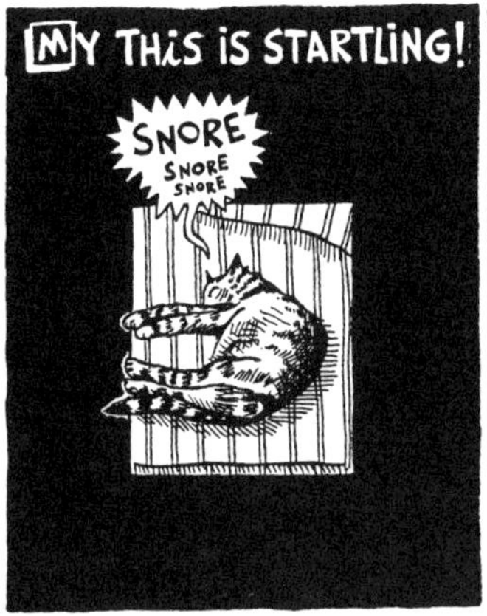
MY THIS IS STARTLING!
SNORE SNORE SNORE

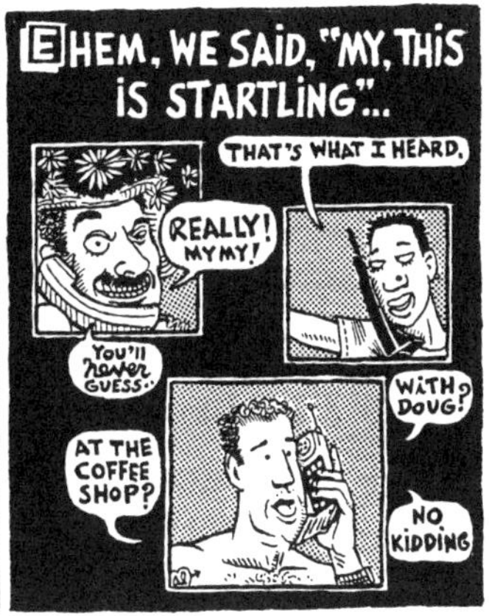
EHEM, WE SAID, "MY, THIS IS STARTLING"...
REALLY! MY MY!
THAT'S WHAT I HEARD.
YOU'LL never GUESS..
AT THE COFFEE SHOP?
WITH DOUG?
NO KIDDING

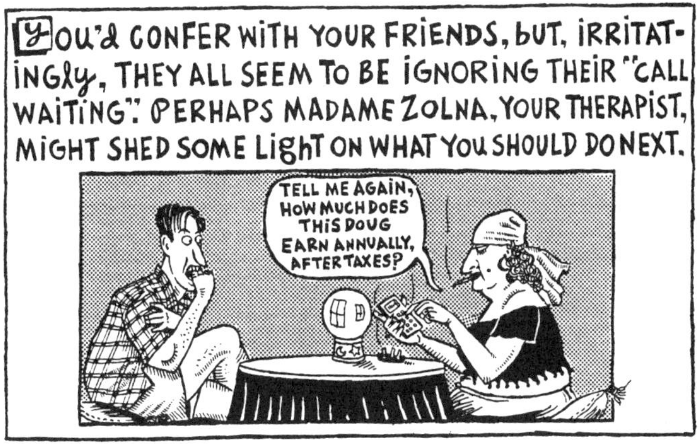
YOU'D CONFER WITH YOUR FRIENDS, BUT, IRRITATINGLY, THEY ALL SEEM TO BE IGNORING THEIR "CALL WAITING". PERHAPS MADAME ZOLNA, YOUR THERAPIST, MIGHT SHED SOME LIGHT ON WHAT YOU SHOULD DO NEXT.
TELL ME AGAIN, HOW MUCH DOES THIS DOUG EARN ANNUALLY, AFTER TAXES?

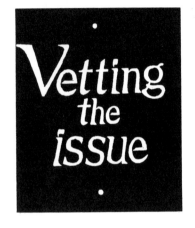

Vetting the issue

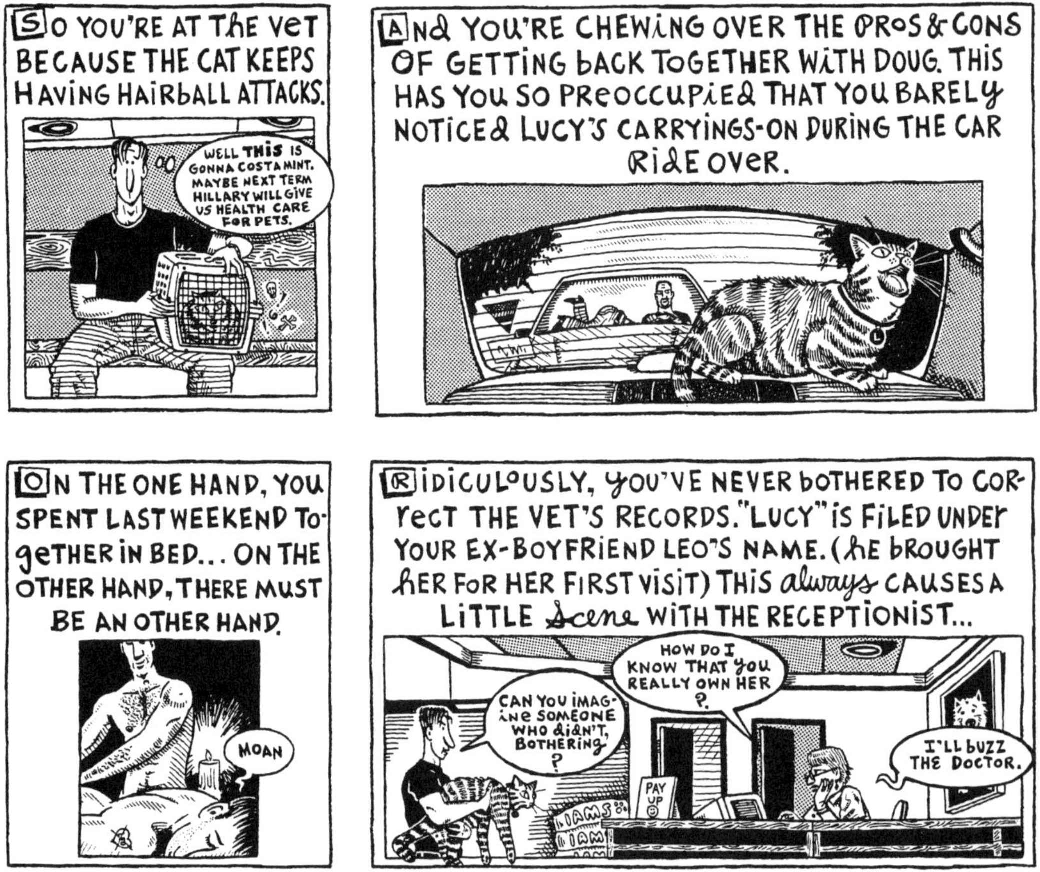
SO YOU'RE AT THE VET BECAUSE THE CAT KEEPS HAVING HAIRBALL ATTACKS.
WELL THIS IS GONNA COST A MINT. MAYBE NEXT TERM HILLARY WILL GIVE US HEALTH CARE FOR PETS.
AND YOU'RE CHEWING OVER THE PROS & CONS OF GETTING BACK TOGETHER WITH DOUG. THIS HAS YOU SO PREOCCUPIED THAT YOU BARELY NOTICED LUCY'S CARRYINGS-ON DURING THE CAR RIDE OVER.
ON THE ONE HAND, YOU SPENT LAST WEEKEND TOGETHER IN BED... ON THE OTHER HAND, THERE MUST BE AN OTHER HAND.
MOAN
RIDICULOUSLY, YOU'VE NEVER BOTHERED TO CORRECT THE VET'S RECORDS. "LUCY" IS FILED UNDER YOUR EX-BOYFRIEND LEO'S NAME. (HE BROUGHT HER FOR HER FIRST VISIT) THIS always CAUSES A LITTLE Scene WITH THE RECEPTIONIST...
CAN YOU IMAGINE SOMEONE WHO DIDN'T, BOTHERING ?
HOW DO I KNOW THAT YOU REALLY OWN HER ?
I'LL BUZZ THE DOCTOR.
PAY UP
IAMS

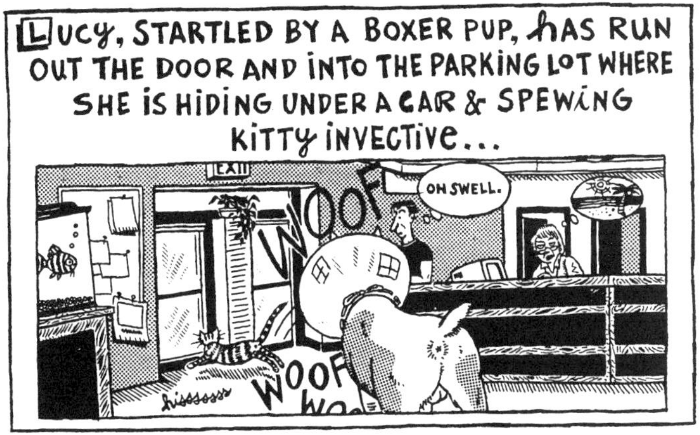
LUCY, STARTLED BY A BOXER PUP, HAS RUN OUT THE DOOR AND INTO THE PARKING LOT WHERE SHE IS HIDING UNDER A CAR & SPEWING KITTY INVECTIVE...
EXIT
OH SWELL.
WOOF
WOOF
hissssss

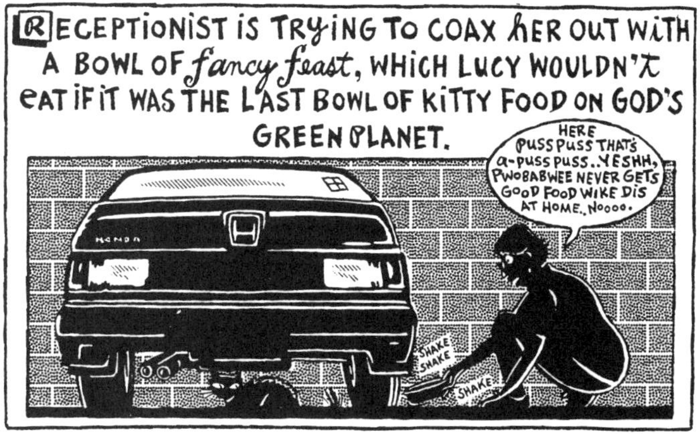
RECEPTIONIST IS TRYING TO COAX HER OUT WITH A BOWL OF fancy feast, WHICH LUCY WOULDN'T EAT IF IT WAS THE LAST BOWL OF KITTY FOOD ON GOD'S GREEN PLANET.
HERE PUSS PUSS THAT'S a-PUSS PUSS.. YESHH, PWOBABWEE NEVER GETS GOOD FOOD WIKE DIS AT HOME.. Noooo.
HONDA
SHAKE
SHAKE
SHAKE

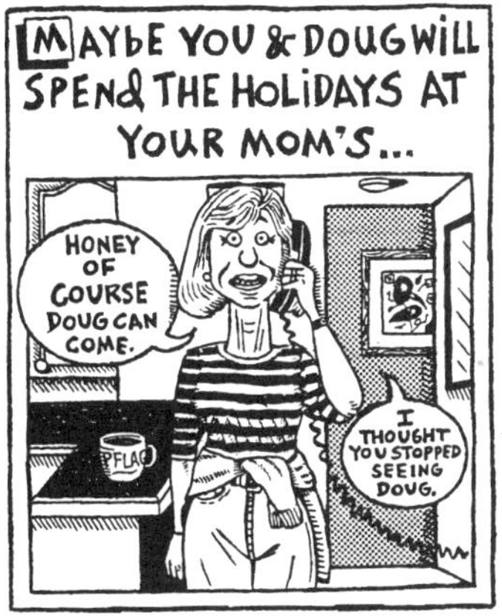
MAYBE YOU & DOUG WILL SPEND THE HOLIDAYS AT YOUR MOM'S...
HONEY OF COURSE DOUG CAN COME.
I THOUGHT YOU STOPPED SEEING DOUG.
PFLAG

HAT
SISTERS
IN
OUTER
SPACE
with *Ethan Green*

God KNOWS YOU LOVE THE HATSISTERS, BUT SHARING A SPACE STATION WITH THEM IS WORKING YOUR NERVES.

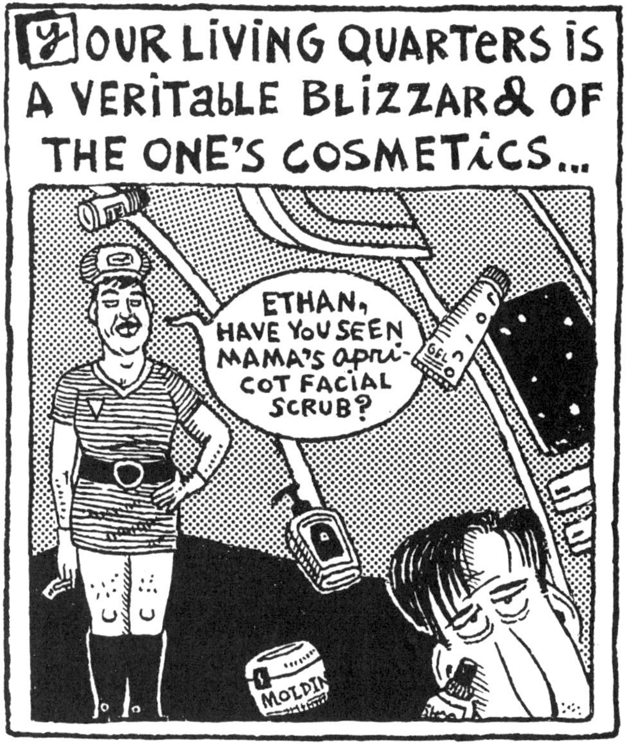
YOUR LIVING QUARTERS IS A VERITABLE BLIZZARD OF THE ONE'S COSMETICS...
ETHAN, HAVE YOU SEEN MAMA'S APRICOT FACIAL SCRUB?
GEL

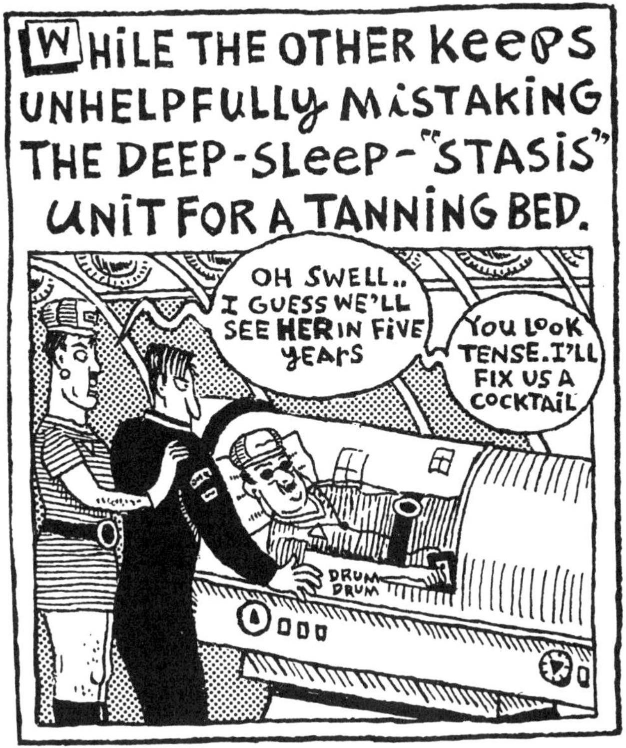
WHILE THE OTHER KEEPS UNHELPFULLY MISTAKING THE DEEP-SLEEP-"STASIS" UNIT FOR A TANNING BED.
OH SWELL.. I GUESS WE'LL SEE HER IN FIVE YEARS
YOU LOOK TENSE. I'LL FIX US A COCKTAIL
DRUM DRUM

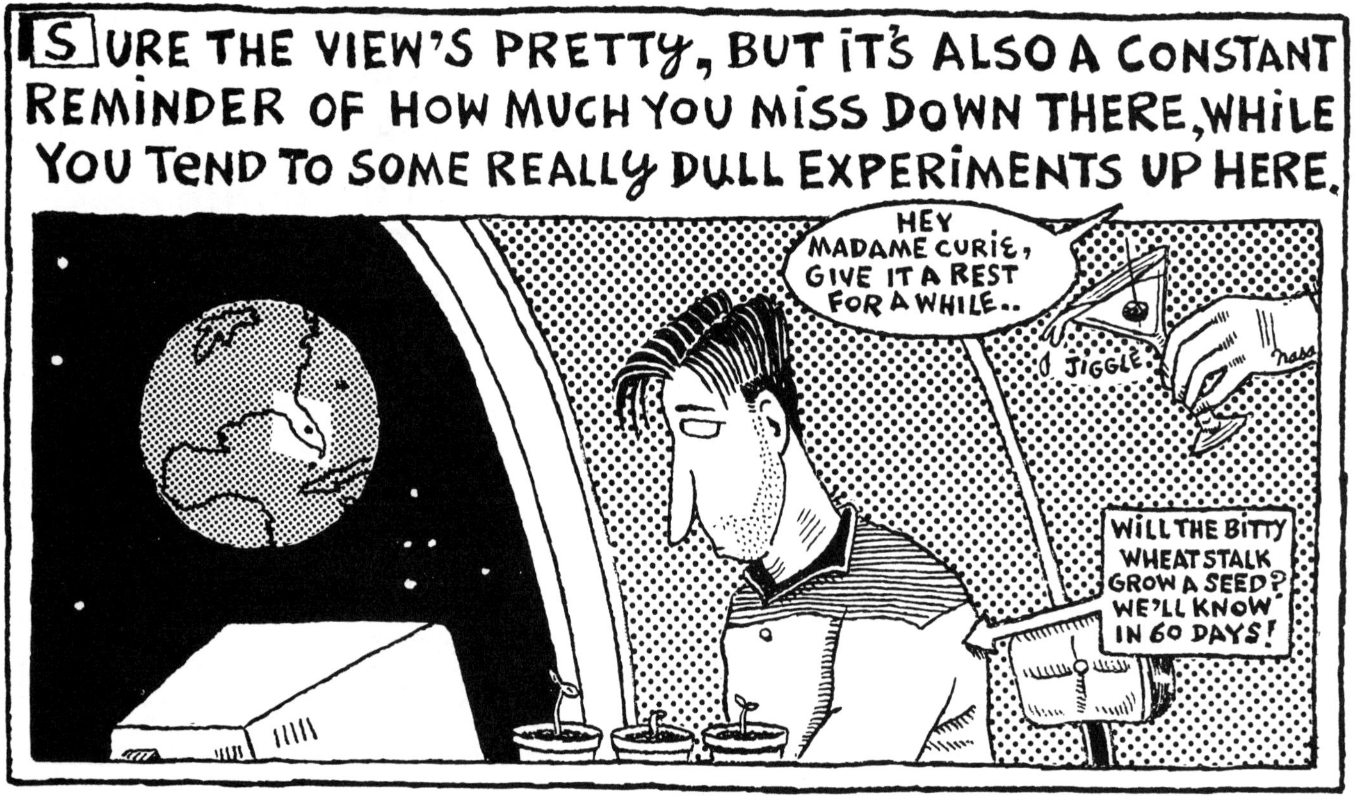
SURE THE VIEW'S PRETTY, BUT IT'S ALSO A CONSTANT REMINDER OF HOW MUCH YOU MISS DOWN THERE, WHILE YOU TEND TO SOME REALLY DULL EXPERIMENTS UP HERE.
HEY MADAME CURIE, GIVE IT A REST FOR A WHILE..
JIGGLE
nasa
WILL THE BITTY WHEAT STALK GROW A SEED? WE'LL KNOW IN 60 DAYS!

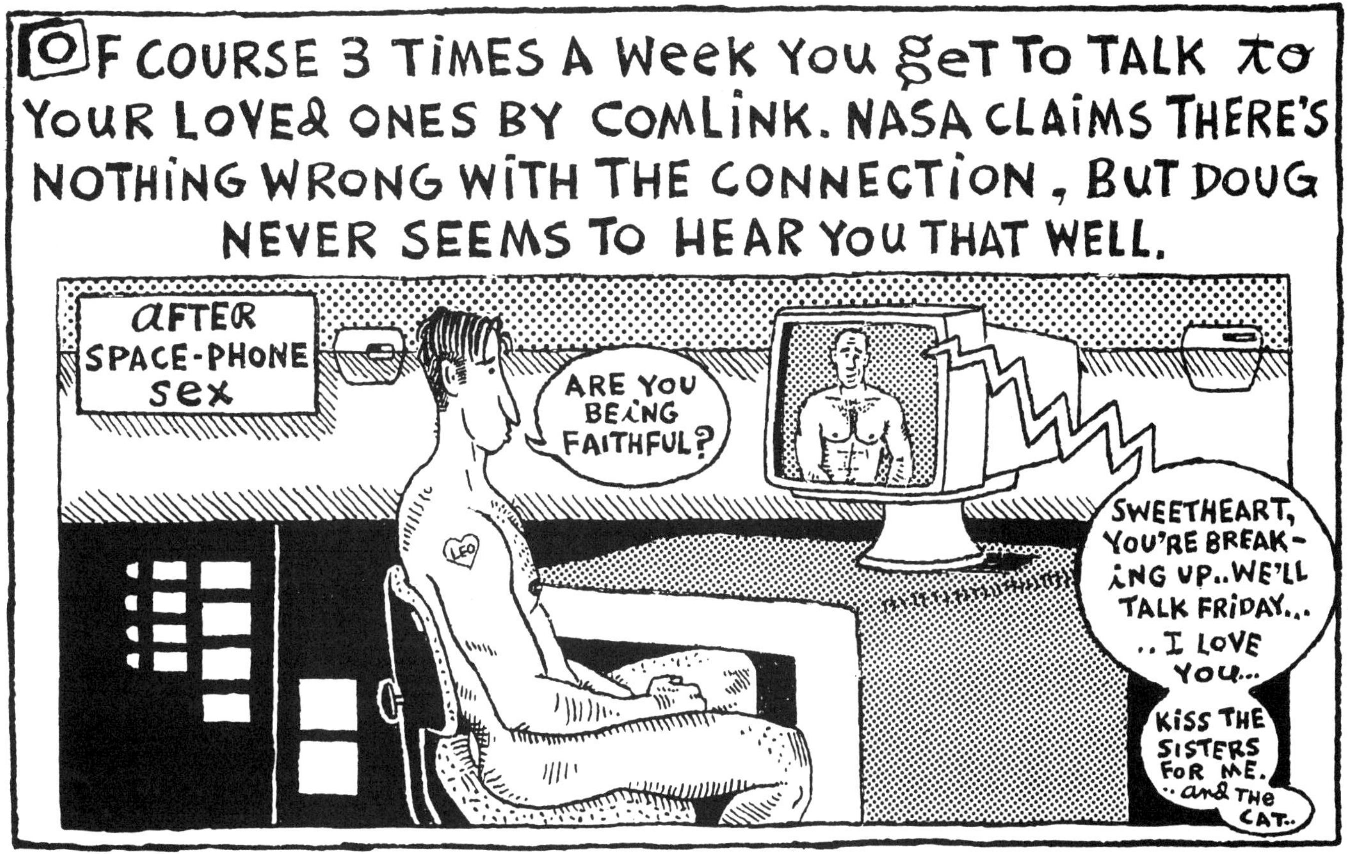
OF COURSE 3 TIMES A WEEK YOU GET TO TALK TO YOUR LOVED ONES BY COMLINK. NASA CLAIMS THERE'S NOTHING WRONG WITH THE CONNECTION, BUT DOUG NEVER SEEMS TO HEAR YOU THAT WELL.
AFTER SPACE-PHONE SEX
ARE YOU BEING FAITHFUL?
LEO
SWEETHEART, YOU'RE BREAK-ING UP.. WE'LL TALK FRIDAY... ..I LOVE YOU...
KISS THE SISTERS FOR ME. ..and THE CAT..

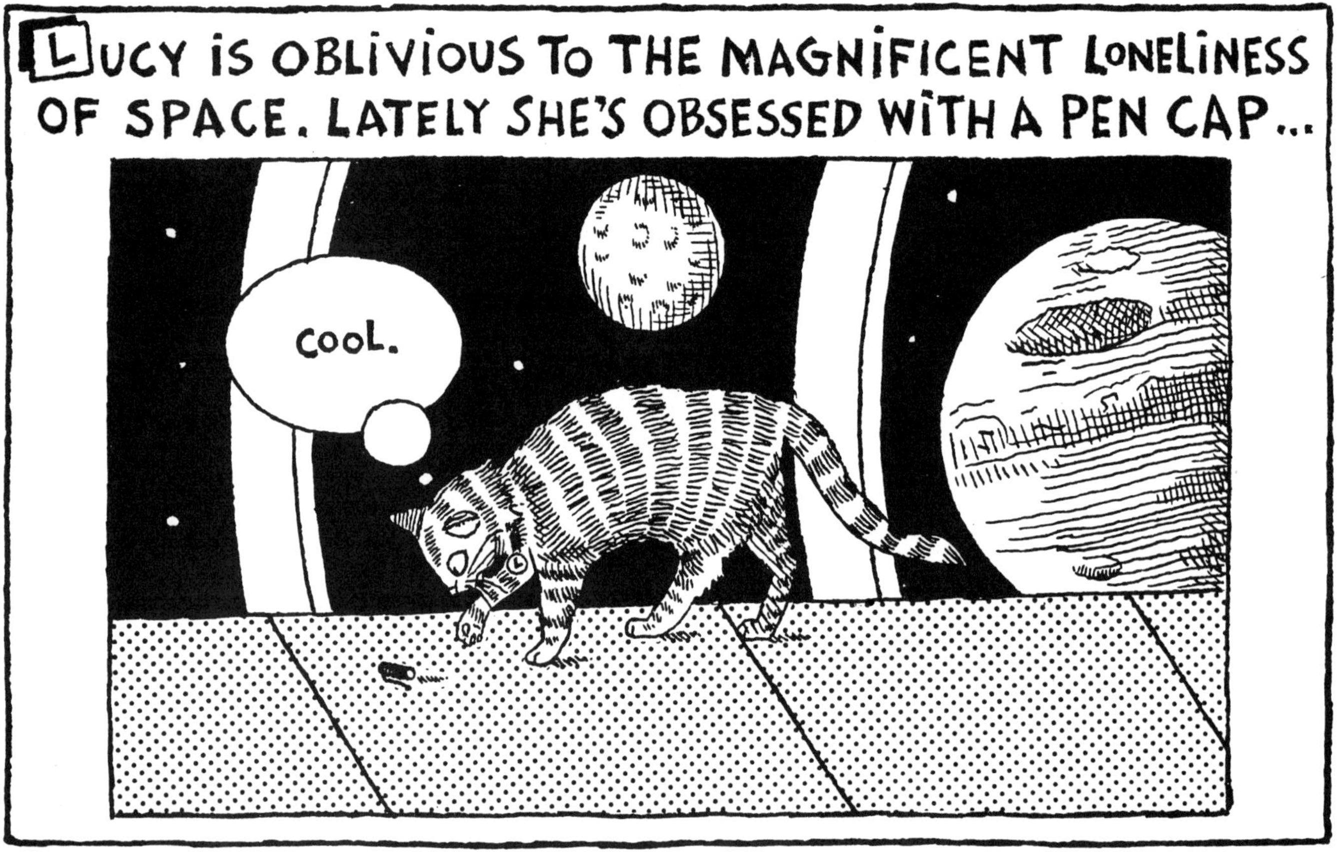
LUCY IS OBLIVIOUS TO THE MAGNIFICENT LONELINESS OF SPACE. LATELY SHE'S OBSESSED WITH A PEN CAP...
COOL.

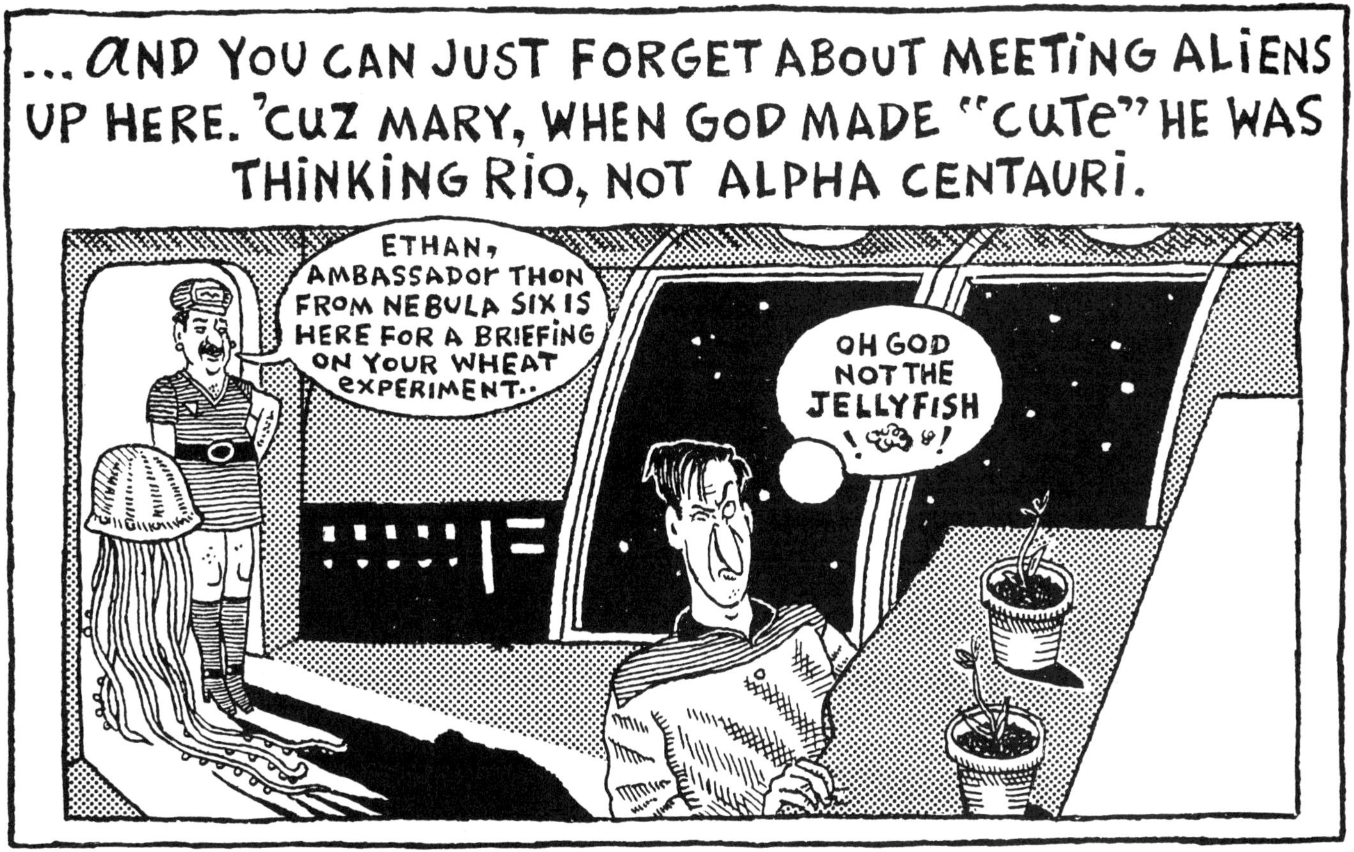
...AND YOU CAN JUST FORGET ABOUT MEETING ALIENS UP HERE. 'CUZ MARY, WHEN GOD MADE "CUTE" HE WAS THINKING RIO, NOT ALPHA CENTAURI.
ETHAN, AMBASSADOR THON FROM NEBULA SIX IS HERE FOR A BRIEFING ON YOUR WHEAT EXPERIMENT..
OH GOD NOT THE JELLYFISH

The Ethan Green
ThanksGiving Smorgasboard O' Fun

RETURN TO ANCESTRAL HOME SLEEP IN WEIRD BED.

MENDACIOUS NEW PET OF YOUR PARENTS. RESENTS YOUR PRESENCE. PLANS TO BITE YOUR HAND...

HUNT DOWN ANCIENT STASH OF "PORNO," DISCOVER IT STILL WORKS..

PlayGirl Feb. 1980
BLUE LAGOON ISSUE
CHRISTOPHER ATKINS. GOSH, IS HE CUTE.

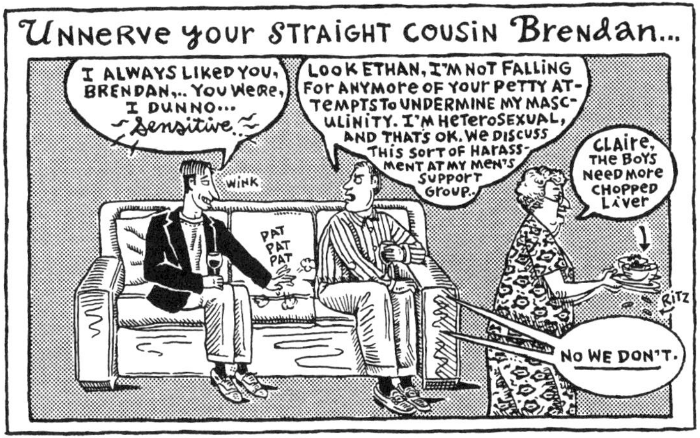
Unnerve your straight cousin Brendan...
I ALWAYS LIKED YOU, BRENDAN,.. YOU WERE, I DUNNO... ~Sensitive..~
WINK
PAT PAT PAT
LOOK ETHAN, I'M NOT FALLING FOR ANYMORE OF YOUR PETTY ATTEMPTS TO UNDERMINE MY MASCULINITY. I'M HETEROSEXUAL, AND THAT'S OK. WE DISCUSS THIS SORT OF HARASSMENT AT MY MEN'S SUPPORT GROUP..
CLAIRE, THE BOYS NEED MORE CHOPPED LIVER
RITZ
NO WE DON'T.

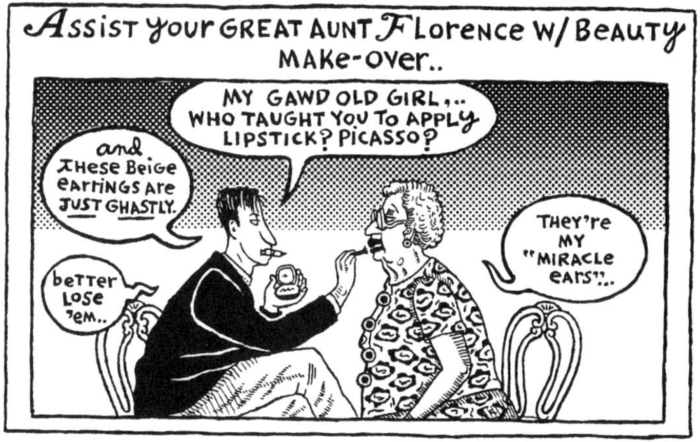
Assist your GREAT AUNT Florence W/ BEAUTY MAKE-OVER..
MY GAWD OLD GIRL,.. WHO TAUGHT YOU TO APPLY LIPSTICK? PICASSO?
and these Beige earrings are JUST GHASTLY.
better lose 'em..
They're MY "MIRACLE ears"..

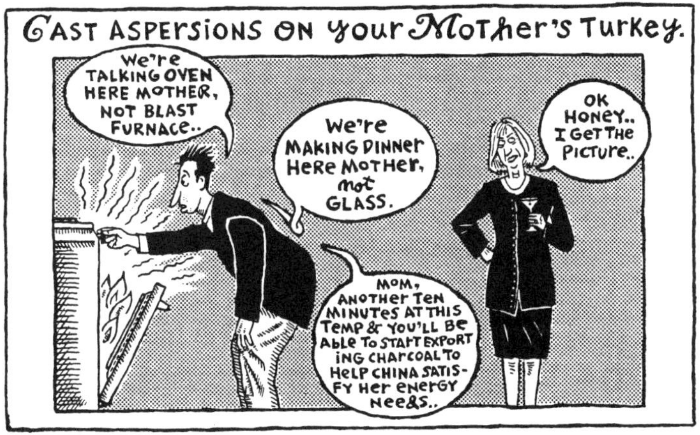
Cast ASPERSIONS ON your Mother's Turkey.
We're TALKING OVEN HERE MOTHER, NOT BLAST FURNACE..
We're MAKING DINNER Here Mother, not GLASS.
OK Honey.. I GET THE PICTURE..
MOM, ANOTHER TEN MINUTES AT THIS TEMP & YOU'LL BE ABLE TO START EXPORTING CHARCOAL TO HELP CHINA SATISFY HER ENERGY NEEDS..

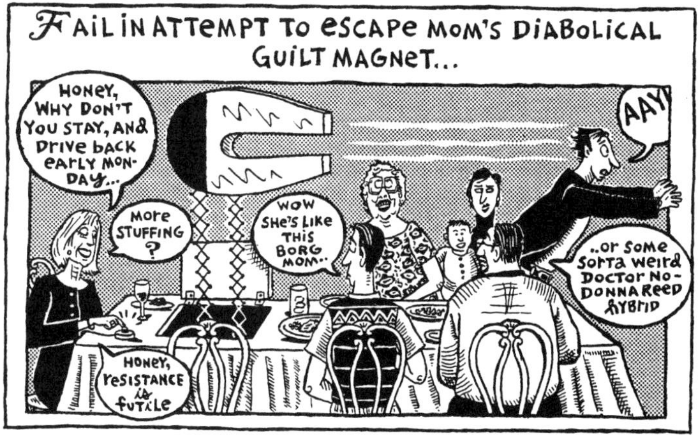
Fail IN ATTEMPT TO escape MOM'S DIABOLICAL GUILT MAGNET...
HONEY, WHY DON'T YOU STAY, AND DRIVE BACK EARLY MONDAY...
AAY
MORE STUFFING ?
WOW SHE'S LIKE THIS BORG MOM..
..or some sorta weird Doctor No-DONNA REED hybrid
HONEY, resistance is futile

ETHAN GREEN'S

Holiday Card Cavalcade.

YOU'RE BIG ON FLIRTING WITH THE MAILMAN

HE MOSTLY IGNORES YOU.

SUPERFICIAL GREETINGS FROM THE X LOVER THAT YOU STILL CARRY A TORCH FOR.

"hey, how's it goin?" Best, —Leo

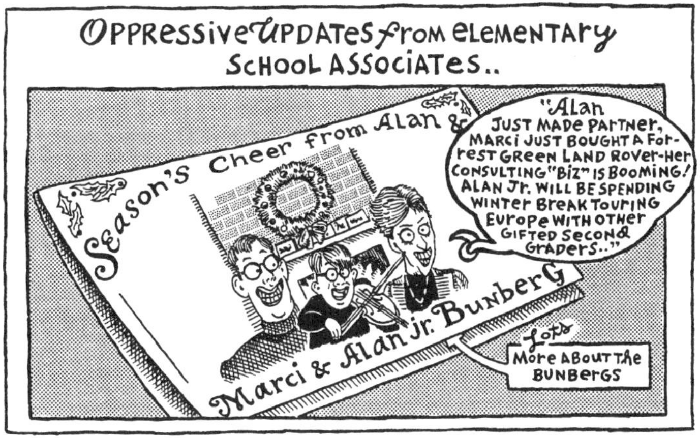
OPPRESSIVE UPDATES from ELEMENTARY SCHOOL ASSOCIATES..
Season's Cheer from Alan &
"Alan JUST MADE PARTNER, MARCI JUST BOUGHT A FOR-REST GREEN LAND ROVER-HER CONSULTING "BIZ" IS BOOMING! ALAN Jr. WILL BE SPENDING WINTER BREAK TOURING EUROPE WITH OTHER GIFTED SECOND GRADERS.."
Marci & Alan Jr. BunberG
Lots More ABOUT THE BUNBERGS

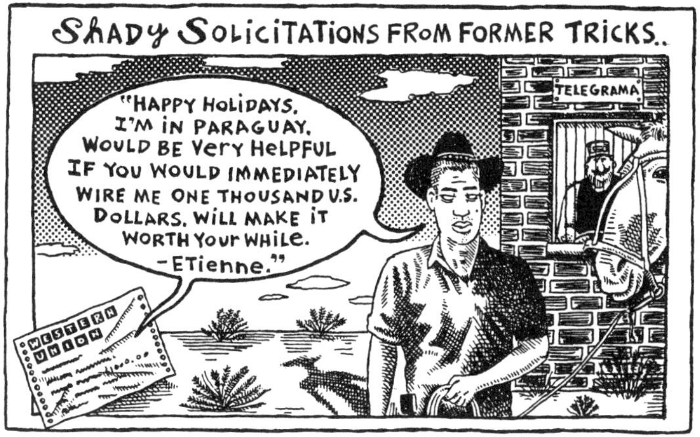
SHADY SOLICITATIONS FROM FORMER TRICKS..
TELEGRAMA
"HAPPY HOLIDAYS. I'M IN PARAGUAY. WOULD BE VERY HELPFUL IF YOU WOULD IMMEDIATELY WIRE ME ONE THOUSAND U.S. DOLLARS. WILL MAKE IT WORTH YOUR WHILE. -ETIENNE."
WESTERN UNION

Eerie Hellos from the Spirit World.

Dear Ethan, as your third grade Teacher, I was well aware of your incipient Homosexuality. You had excellent Penmanship. Male homosexuals often do you see...

Sincerely, M. Hansford. (deceased)

Smarmy Salutations from Local Politicians.

"WHILE NOT GAY OURSELVES, MY WIFE (NEWS ANCHOR DAPHNEY HANDY) & I BELIEVE Y'ALL SHOULD BE TOLERATED, & SHOULD WRITE WHOPPING CHECKS TO MY CAMPAIGN COMMITTEE AS OFTEN AS POSSIBLE.."

Joyeux Noel! STATE SENATOR JIM HANDY

Special Introductory Holiday Offers..

A HOLIDAY MESSAGE FROM DANN. R. JONES, FOUNDER, MIDWESTERNGUY SELF HELP PROGRAM

IS YOUR LOVE LIFE NON EXISTANT? YOUR JOB A BORE? YOUR LOOKS FADING

CUZ YOU AIN'T TWENTY ONE NO MORE? WELL FRIEND, MY MIDWESTERNGUY METHOD'LL CHANGE YOUR SORRY LIFE! SPECIAL INTRODUCTORY OFFER JUST $79!

GUYS DIG THESE HATS TRUST ME!

BOYFRIEND CATCHING GURU DANN R. JONES IN FABULOUS SYDNEY AUSTRALIA..

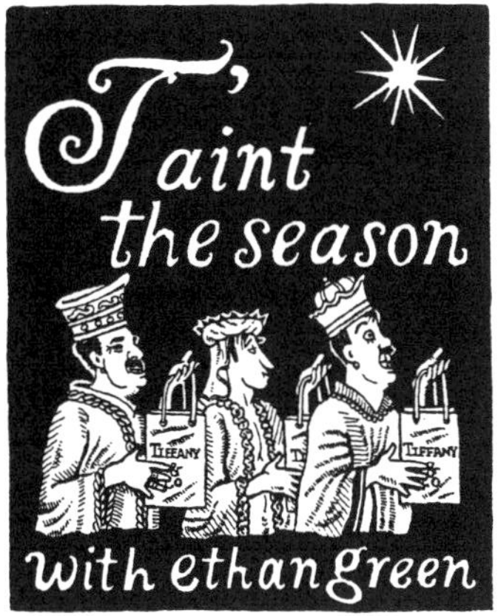
'Taint the season
with ethan green
TIFFANY
TIFFANY

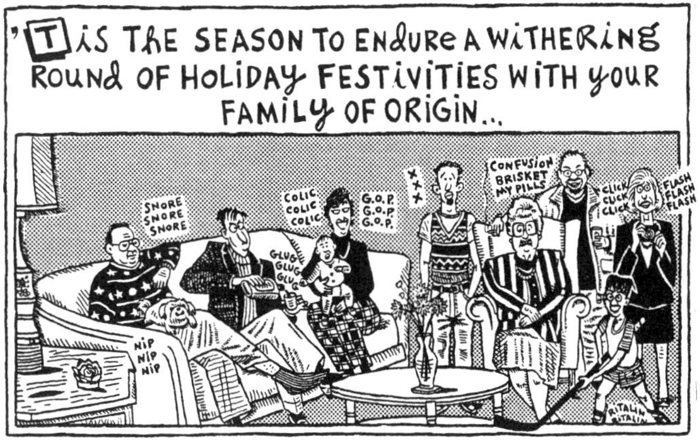
'TIS THE SEASON TO ENDURE A WITHERING ROUND OF HOLIDAY FESTIVITIES WITH YOUR FAMILY OF ORIGIN...
SNORE SNORE SNORE
NIP NIP NIP
GLUG GLUG GLUG
COLIC COLIC COLIC
G.O.P. G.O.P. G.O.P.
XXX
CONFUSION BRISKET MY PILLS
CLICK CLICK CLICK
FLASH FLASH FLASH
RITALIN RITALIN

...WHILE BACK AT (your) HOME, YOUR FAMILY OF CHOICE ENJOYS A RAUCUS WEEKEND OF SPIKED EGGNOG AND MOVIE RENTALS...

YOU & DOUG ARE SLEEPING TOGETHER AGAIN. HE'S TAKING THE TRAIN OUT TO YOUR PARENTS' PLACE ON FRIDAY.

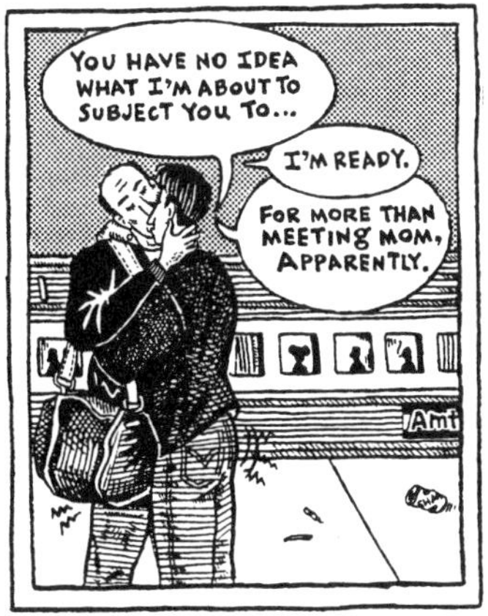
YOU HAVE NO IDEA WHAT I'M ABOUT TO SUBJECT YOU TO...
I'M READY.
FOR MORE THAN MEETING MOM, APPARENTLY.

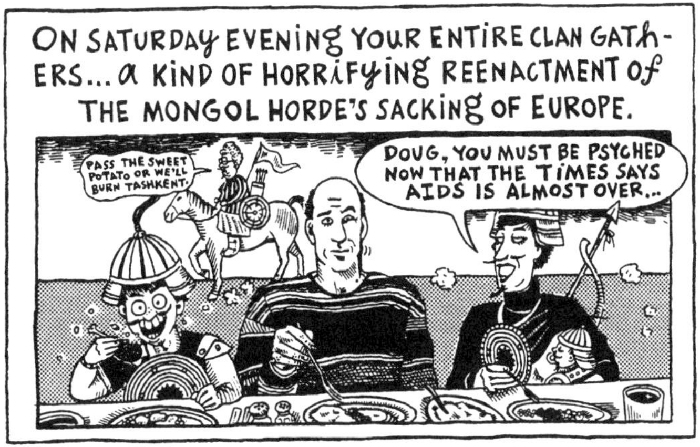
ON SATURDAY EVENING YOUR ENTIRE CLAN GATH-ERS... A KIND OF HORRIFYING REENACTMENT OF THE MONGOL HORDE'S SACKING OF EUROPE.
PASS THE SWEET POTATO OR WE'LL BURN TASHKENT.
DOUG, YOU MUST BE PSYCHED NOW THAT THE TIMES SAYS AIDS IS ALMOST OVER...

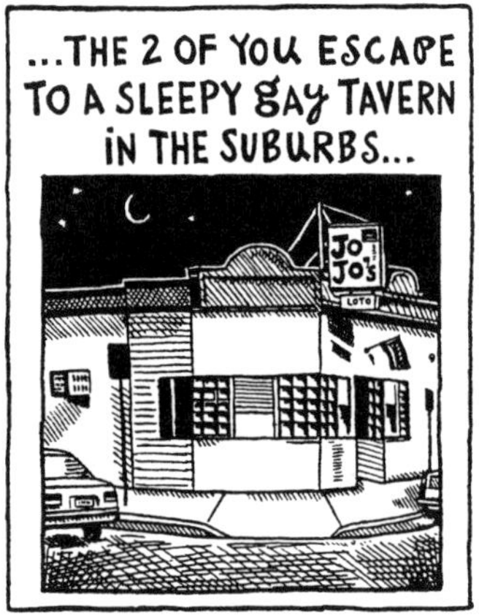
...THE 2 OF YOU ESCAPE TO A SLEEPY GAY TAVERN IN THE SUBURBS...
JO JO'S

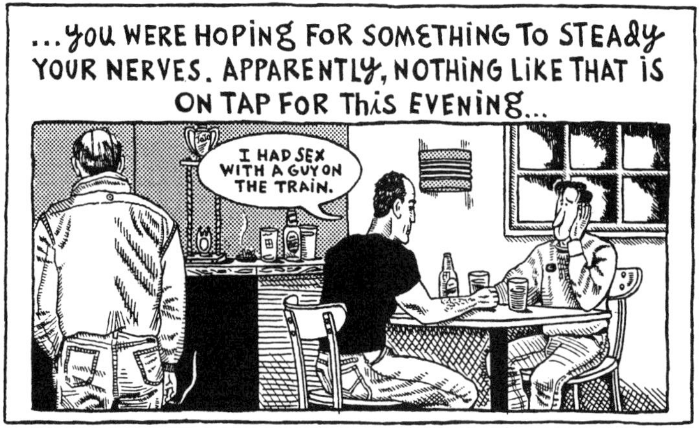
...YOU WERE HOPING FOR SOMETHING TO STEADY YOUR NERVES. APPARENTLY, NOTHING LIKE THAT IS ON TAP FOR THIS EVENING...
I HAD SEX WITH A GUY ON THE TRAIN.

Mostly Monogamy

We rejoin ETHAN & DOUG AS THEY ATTEMPT TO PROCESS DOUG'S RAILWAY TRANSGRESSION
DOUG, THERE'S LIKE THIS BIG TORAH FLOATING ABOVE THE HOUSE..
I DON'T KNOW WHY I DID IT.. I JUST DID... I LOVE YOU. NOT SOME TRICK ON A TRAIN.. WHY IS IT SO IMPORTANT ?! IT'S JUST SEX... JUST SOME ANIMAL NEED. IT MEANT NOTHING...
GLARE
THIS WEEK'S LATEST CRITIQUE OF BEAUTY WORSHIP IN GAY MALE CULTURE WITH PECS & ABS ON COVER...

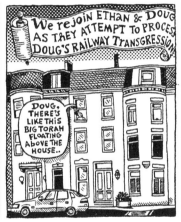

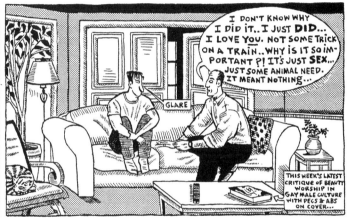

SO WHAT'S YOUR BOTTOM LINE HERE? IF WE ARE GOING TO BE TOGETHER, WE ARE GOING TO HAVE AN OPEN RELATIONSHIP?
OH GOD ETHAN, YOU MAKE IT SOUND LIKE I PLAN ON INSTALLING A REVOLVING DOOR AT THE FOOT OF THE BED...
WELL I WOULDN'T WANT TO GET IN THE WAY OF ONE OF THOSE animal needs...
BEFORE, WHEN WE WERE TOGETHER, WE WERE MONOGAMOUS AND IT DIDN'T WORK..
SILLY ME. I THOUGHT THAT HAD TO DO WITH LOST T-CELLS, NOT WANDERING EYES.
GLARE GLARE
PURR PURR PURR PURR
WITHOUT LOYALTY

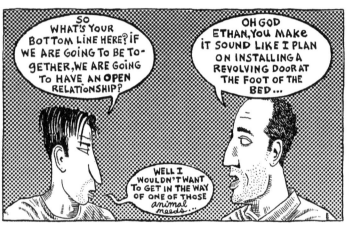

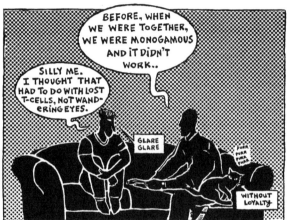

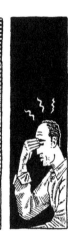

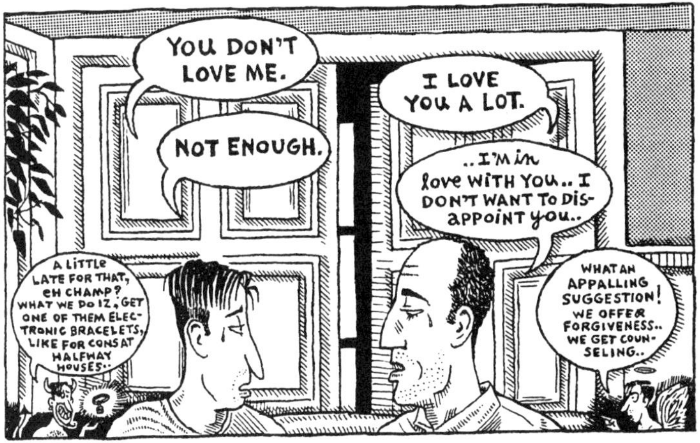
YOU DON'T LOVE ME.
I LOVE YOU A LOT.
NOT ENOUGH.
..I'M in love WITH YOU.. I DON'T WANT TO DISAPPOINT you..
A LITTLE LATE FOR THAT, EH CHAMP? WHAT WE DO IZ, GET ONE OF THEM ELECTRONIC BRACELETS, LIKE FOR CONS AT HALFWAY HOUSES..
WHAT AN APPALLING SUGGESTION! WE OFFER FORGIVENESS.. WE GET COUNSELING..

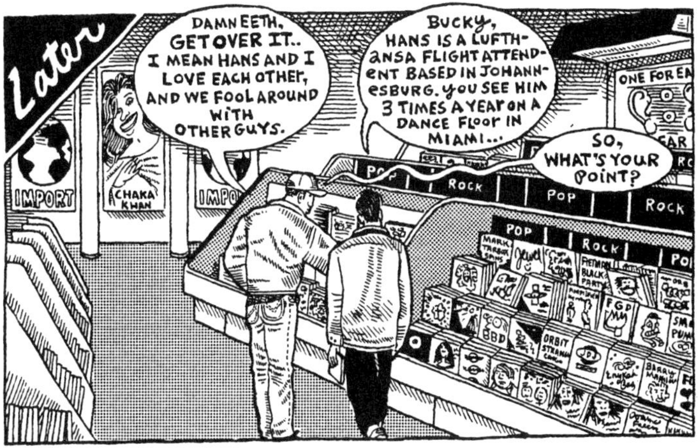
Later
DAMN EETH, GET OVER IT.. I MEAN HANS AND I LOVE EACH OTHER, AND WE FOOL AROUND WITH OTHER GUYS.
BUCKY, HANS IS A LUFTHANSA FLIGHT ATTENDENT BASED IN JOHANNESBURG. YOU SEE HIM 3 TIMES A YEAR ON A DANCE FLOOR IN MIAMI...
SO, WHAT'S YOUR POINT?
IMPORT
CHAKA KHAN
POP
ROCK

The

Gay Man's Guide

to

ALL YOUR RELATIONSHIPS

SISTERS are your dearest friends. The ones with whom you share history, humiliations and hotel rooms. Sisters are who you couldn't live without. Sisters are who you imagine bawling at your funeral.

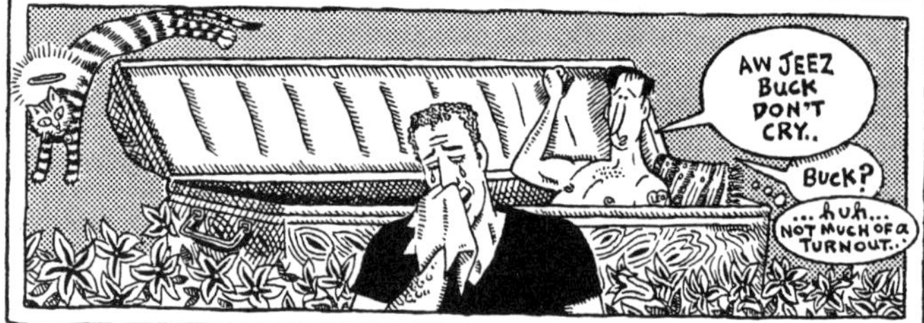
AW JEEZ BUCK DON'T CRY..
BUCK?
...huh... NOT MUCH OF A TURNOUT..

AUNTIES are who dote on you, get you to eat something on occasion, and have pasts crammed with stories that make your wildest adventures pale by comparison.

IT WAS LABOR DAY AT THE OLD TOWN ART FAIR, 1978. YOUR AUNTY HERE INEBRIATED HERSELF AND WOUND UP ENJOYING A LOVELY TRIO OF EBONY MEN ON A SAILBOAT ONE KEPT IN BELMONT HARBOR...

THREE?

NOT COUNTING THE HARBORMASTER... C'MON, SON, EAT...

EX HUSBANDS are family. And like everyone else who falls under that designation, they are loved and not live-with-able.

OH JOY. THE PRODIGAL FIRST BOY-FRIEND re-TURNETA...

ETHAN, YOU KNOW I NEVER REALLY STOPPED LOVING *caring about* YOU. LET'S GIVE IT ANOTHER SHOT...

LEO, CALL ME WHEN YOU GET a PHONE...

35

GIRLFRIENDS are straight women that you met in college and never stopped adoring.

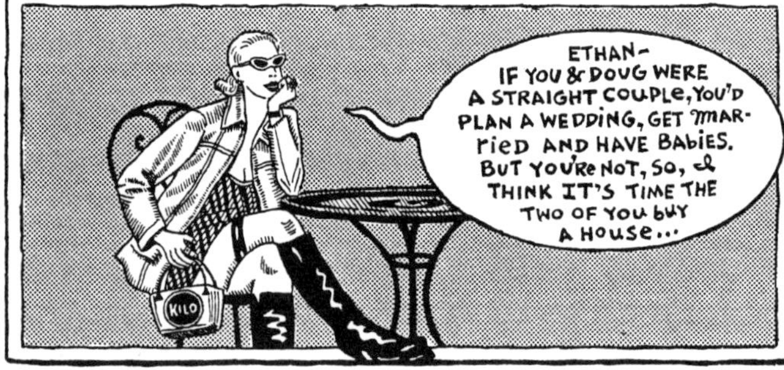
KILO
ETHAN- IF YOU & DOUG WERE A STRAIGHT COUPLE, YOU'D PLAN A WEDDING, GET MAR-RIED AND HAVE BABIES. BUT YOU'RE NOT, SO, I THINK IT'S TIME THE TWO OF YOU BUY A HOUSE...

CUZINS are close friends living in remote locations. Cuzins are who you call and who you visit.

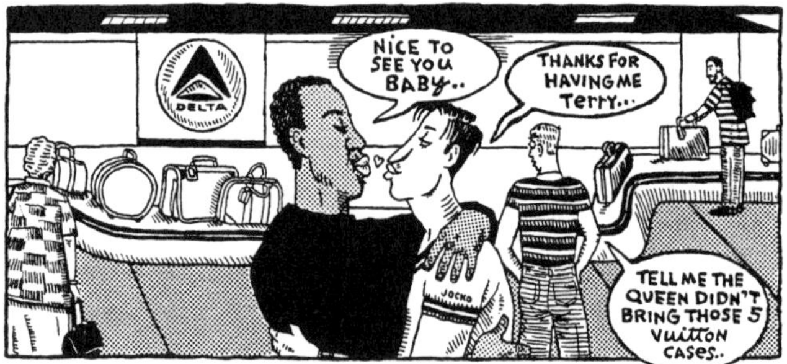
DELTA
NICE TO SEE YOU BABY..
THANKS FOR HAVING ME Terry...
JOCKO
TELL ME THE QUEEN DIDN'T BRING THOSE 5 Vuitton CASES..

KISSING CUZINS are close friends living in remote locations. Kissing Cuzins are who you call, visit, and occasionally end up in bed with.

FOR SOMEONE WHO BROUGHT A HALF DOZEN SUITCASES, Y'ALL DON'T WEAR A LOT OF CLOTHES.

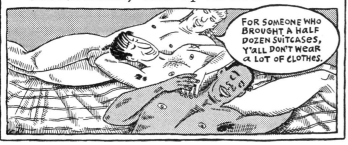

NEIGHBORS are the lesbians with whom you share cups of coffee, tales of pet parenting, and the occasional cross cultural exchange.

YOU BOYS NEED TO GET A WHOLE LOT MORE INFORMED ABOUT WOMEN'S HEALTH ISSUES...
CHARLOTTE, I'VE ENDURED A QUEER AMERICAN BOYHOOD, THE STRESSES OF COMING OUT, THE PREMATURE DEATH OF MANY FRIENDS, DON'T YOU THINK I'VE EARNED THE RIGHT NOT TO BE CALLED BOY?
YES, COME TO THINK OF IT, I GUESS SO...
thanks WHAT TIME DID YOU SAY THAT BREAST CANCER RALLY WAS?

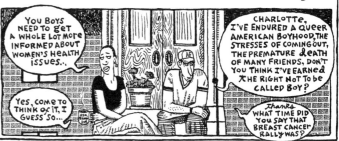

OLD TRICKS are the guys you said you'd hook up with again, but didn't. Old Tricks can be gracious, "It was fun," or pissy.

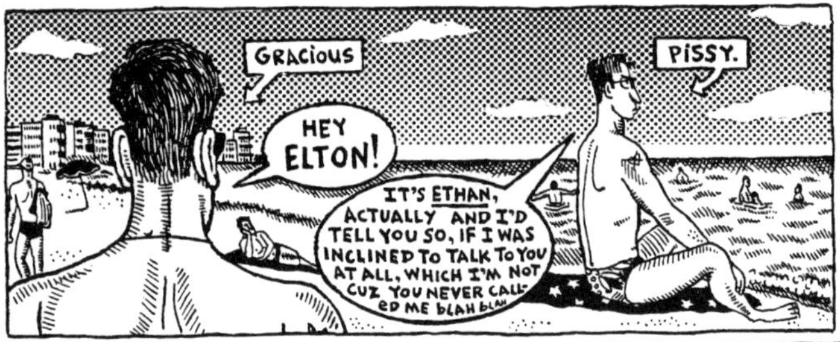
GRACIOUS
PISSY.
HEY ELTON!
IT'S ETHAN, ACTUALLY AND I'D TELL YOU SO, IF I WAS INCLINED TO TALK TO YOU AT ALL, WHICH I'M NOT CUZ YOU NEVER CALLED ME BLAH BLAH

CURRENT TRICKS are who you rush home to check for messages from. Current Tricks are the subject of Sisterly indulgence and Old Trick Fury.

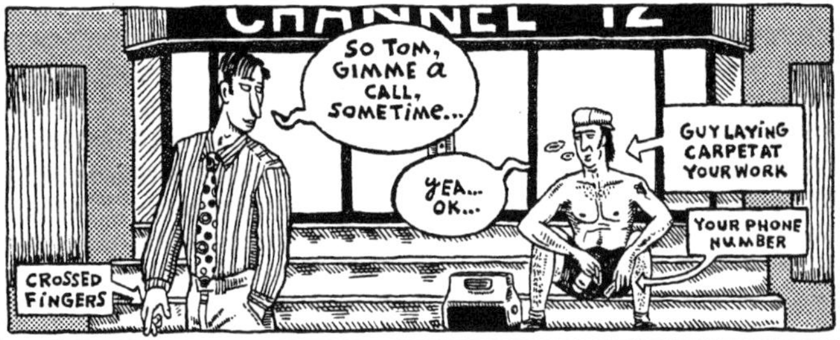
SO TOM, GIMME A CALL, SOMETIME...
YEA... OK...
GUY LAYING CARPET AT YOUR WORK
YOUR PHONE NUMBER
CROSSED FINGERS

SOULMATES are the people who your body talks your mind into believing share all sorts of cosmic connections with you, when in fact they're just people your body wants to sleep with.

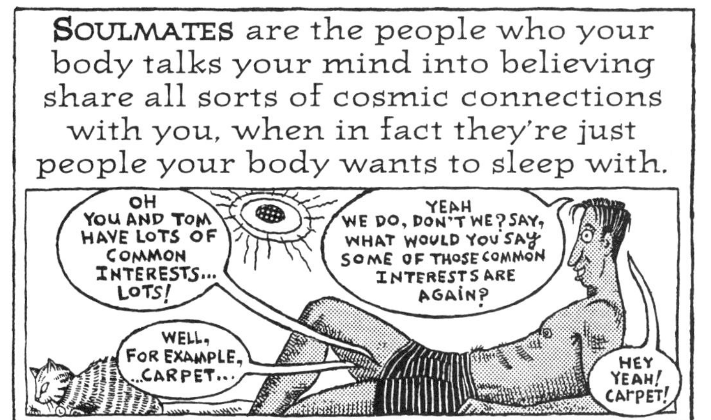

OH YOU AND TOM HAVE LOTS OF COMMON INTERESTS... LOTS!
YEAH WE DO, DON'T WE? SAY, WHAT WOULD YOU SAY SOME OF THOSE COMMON INTERESTS ARE AGAIN?
WELL, FOR EXAMPLE, ..CARPET...
HEY YEAH! CARPET!

Ethan Green in
12
9
3
6
9 to 5
ETHAN GREEN HAS GONE OUT AND GOTTEN HIMSELF A NEW JOB...
WHADDYA MEAN "NEW"?
WHO KNEW HE HAD AN OLD JOB?..
KVETCHING, ALONE, DOESN'T PAY WELL APPARENTLY.
YEA, WELL, YOU SHOULD SEE WHAT THIS PAYS..
BOB & ROD'S GUIDE TO SPLITSVILLE

HE'S THE NEW PERSONAL ASSISTANT FOR MONTY POOLE, NEWSCENTER 12'S LEGENDARY WEATHERMAN.
FABULOUS WEEKEND WEATHER !!!
EVERY SENTIENT BEING IN THE TRI-STATE AREA KNOWS MONTY'S A BIG OLD QUEEN... MONTY DOES NOT KNOW THEY KNOW, HOWEVER.
MY WHOLE FAMILY WATCHES MONTY EVERY NIGHT!
WELL, HILLARY AND CHELSEA AND I WATCH MONTY ALSO.
I LOVE THE OLD POOF.

ONE OF THE GUYS ON THE STORM-TRACKING STAFF MIGHT BE GAY ALSO. HE EXPLAINED TO ETHAN ABOUT FRIDAYS.

GLASSY EYED, FIRST DAY OF WORK LOOK

YOU MONTY'S NEW ASSISTANT?

YEH.

PULL UP A CHAIR SON...

TAP TAP TAP

THAT'S THE DAY THAT MONTY'S SHIRTS GO TO THE LAUNDRY. EXTRA STARCH, BOXED.

IT'S 10AM, I SHOULD BE WATCHING ROSIE O'DONNEL...

INCOMING ZOMBIE FEHGELA WITH SHIRTS

Golden TOUCH CLEANERS

SHIRTS

SUEDE LEATHER CLEAN

OPEN

GREEN SOUVLA

KASICH SHORT CAFE

42

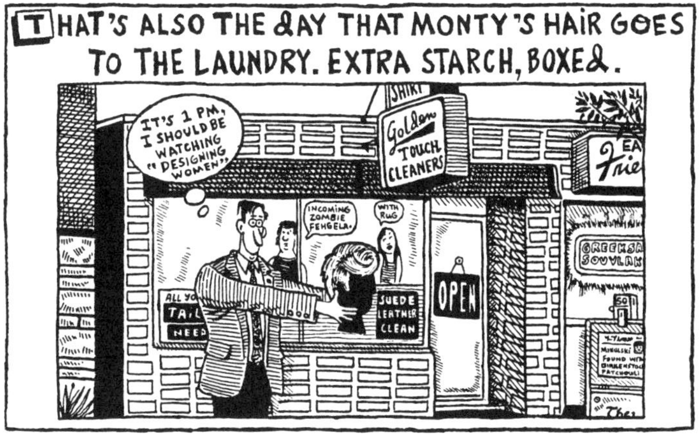
THAT'S ALSO THE DAY THAT MONTY'S HAIR GOES TO THE LAUNDRY. EXTRA STARCH, BOXED.
IT'S 1 PM, I SHOULD BE WATCHING "DESIGNING WOMEN"
INCOMING ZOMBIE FEHGELA.
WITH RUG
SHIRT
Golden TOUCH CLEANERS
SUEDE LEATHER CLEAN
OPEN

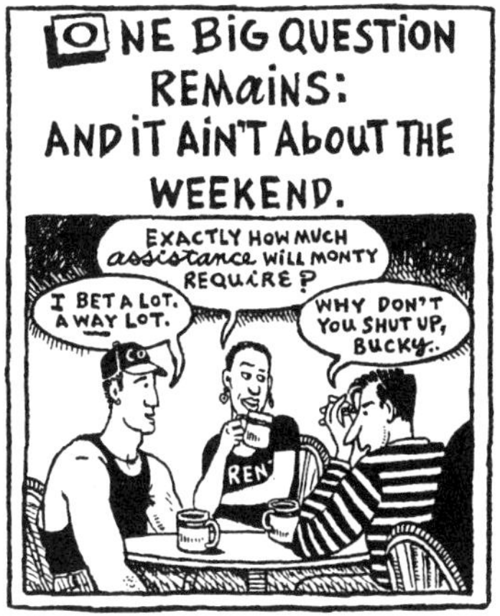
ONE BIG QUESTION REMAINS: AND IT AIN'T ABOUT THE WEEKEND.
EXACTLY HOW MUCH assistance WILL MONTY REQUIRE?
I BET A LOT. A WAY LOT.
WHY DON'T YOU SHUT UP, BUCKY.

A Few Weekends back Doug lost his erection while he and the hero of our story were making love...

IT'S NO BIG DEAL, SWEETHEART.
PLEASE DON'T GET ALL FREAKED OUT ABOUT IT.
JEEZ-mine DOESN'T WORK LOTS OF TIMES
..WELL, NOT EXACTLY "LOTS" OF TIMES I MEAN, WIT YOU, UH- BABBLE, BABBLE

I'VE BEEN FEELING KIND OF LISTLESS, LATELY...
LISTLESS AS IN BORED? OR AS IN NO ENERGY?
AS IN SLUGGISH.
SLUGGISH AS IN SLOW-MOVING? OR AS IN WET AND SLIMEY?
AS IN FLUISH.
FLUISH LIKE ACHY? OR FLUISH LIKE FEVERY?
LIKE HEADACHEY. LIKE YOU ARE MAKING ME HEADACHEY!
CALL JASON
I DUNNO...
CALL HIM

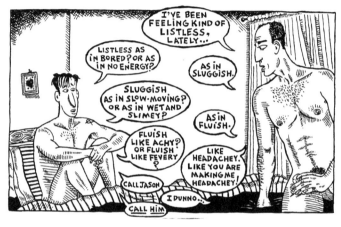

SO? WHAT'd HE SAY?

THAT IT HAS TO DO WITH STRESS FROM STARTING THE WOODWORKING BUSINESS & NOTHING TO DO WITH THE VIRUS..

DID'J'a TELL HIM THAT YOU'VE BEEN TAKING THAT CREEPY HERB YOU GOT FROM PICANO?

YES... AND HE SAYS IT'S FINE.

MAYBE THAT STUFF DOESN'T MIX WELL WITH THE CRIXIVAN..

SWEETHEART, GO TO MEDICAL SCHOOL, PASS YOUR BOARDS, DO YOUR RESIDENCY AND THEN I'LL TAKE YOUR ADVICE. UNTIL THEN I'M LISTENING TO JASON.

I'M GONNA TAKE A NAP.

45

1 WEEK LATER
INSIDE DOUG'S HEAD:
HEY DOUGIE!
IT'S US! YOUR LIBIDO!
WE'RE BACK!
HONK HONK
INSIDE DOUG'S BED:
SEX DRIVE'S BACK..
SWEETHEART IT'S THE 4Th TIME YOU'VE WANTED TO FUCK ME THIS AFTERNOON
NIBBLE
I'M BEGINNING TO MISS THE SEX DRIVE'S VACA-TION..
Still Later...
SINCE WHEN DO YOU GET OFF ON SHAVING?
I DUNNO.. THOSE HERBS FROM PICANO MUST HAVE a KINKY SIDE EFFECT..
BUZZZ
tomorrow at work...
IT'S NICE PLEASING DOUG, BUT Jeez, IT'S GONNA be AN itchy week..
WHATS TH' MATTER GREEN, ANTS IN YER PANTS? HA HAHA WHEEZE WHEEZE Wheeze
GOOD ONE MONTY.
WHERE'S TONITE'S SCRIPT?
COMING.
CHOP CHOP

IT'S RAINING *Weather* MEN

PART OF YOUR NEW JOB AT CHANNEL 12 INVOLVES USING THE STATION'S SOPHISTICATED METEOROLOGICAL EQUIPMENT TO WORK UP MONTY POOLE'S DAILY FORECAST..
TELEPHONE
ON THE DAY THAT YOU WERE BORN THE ANGELS GOT TOGETHER
WEATHER SERVICE PHONE #

THE STATION HAS OPTED FOR A LEMONADE-FROM-LEMONS APPROACH TO THE FACT THAT HIS FORECAST IS NEVER RIGHT...
GET IT WRONG with MONTY
12
VOLVO

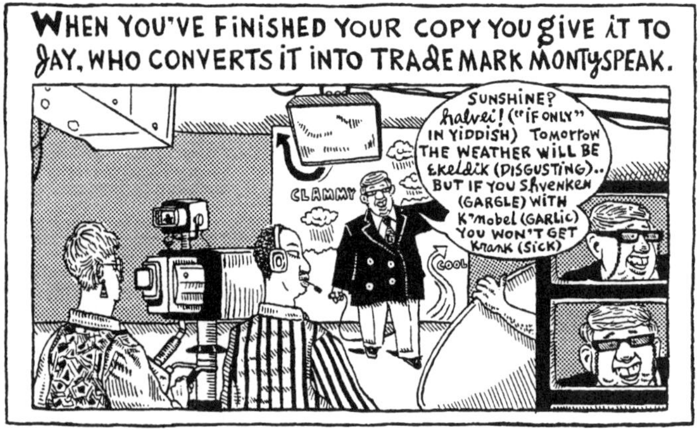
WHEN YOU'VE FINISHED YOUR COPY YOU GIVE IT TO JAY, WHO CONVERTS IT INTO TRADEMARK MONTYSPEAK.
SUNSHINE? halvei! ("IF ONLY" IN YIDDISH) TOMORROW THE WEATHER WILL BE Ekeldik (DISGUSTING).. BUT IF YOU Shvenken (GARGLE) WITH K'nobel (GARLIC) YOU WON'T GET Krank (SICK)
CLAMMY
COOL

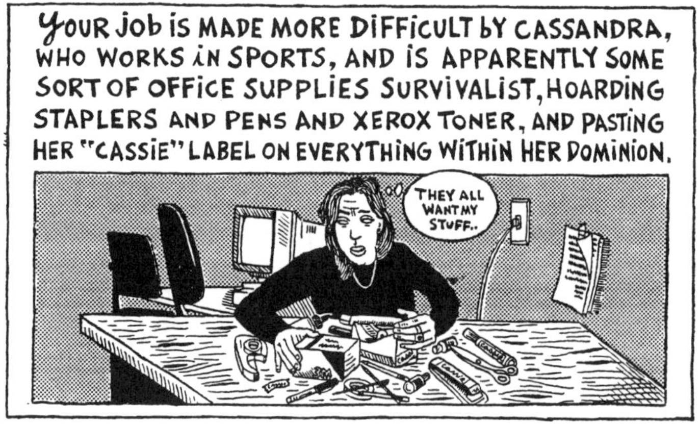
YOUR JOB IS MADE MORE DIFFICULT BY CASSANDRA, WHO WORKS IN SPORTS, AND IS APPARENTLY SOME SORT OF OFFICE SUPPLIES SURVIVALIST, HOARDING STAPLERS AND PENS AND XEROX TONER, AND PASTING HER "CASSIE" LABEL ON EVERYTHING WITHIN HER DOMINION.
THEY ALL WANT MY STUFF..

MONTY SPENDS HIS DAYS 25 MINUTES FROM THE STATION ON HIS HUGE SUBURBAN RANCH PLAYING COMPUTER BACKGAMMON OVER THE INTERNET WITH HIS WEATHERMEN GIRLFRIENDS.

GARY GREENWAY in VANCOUVER.

"DAL" DIGBY in PHOENIX

CURT CROSBY in WEST PALM

AT 3 PM YOU PICK HIM UP AND BRING HIM BACK TO THE STATION. HE'S EITHER PILLY OR EXPANSIVE, DEPENDING ON HOW HIS GAME WENT..

THAT DAL DIGBY IS A SHYSTER!

YES MONTY

HER FRANK LLOYD WRIGHT LOOK.

MOST DAYS YOU EAT LUNCH WITH JAY, WHOSE KINDNESS PREVENTS HIM FROM TELLING YOU HOW RIDICULOUS HE THINKS YOUR PROBLEMS ARE.

SO I DON'T THINK DOUG LOVES ME ENOUGH.

OH LORD HERE WE GO..

49

Ethan has agreed to dogsit for Abby while her moms, Liza & Beth spend two weeks camping on Vieques...

Leading us to present this entirely non comprehensive accounting of the...→

Criminals of Doggiewalk Park

SAYS "HE *never* ACTS THIS WAY" every MORNING AFTER her DOG BITES SOMEONE.

YAP YAP YAP

PEES ON his OWN THROWING TOY...

REFUSES TO OBEY HIS DAD EVERY SINGLE TIME ANOTHER DOG-PARENT IS WATCHING.

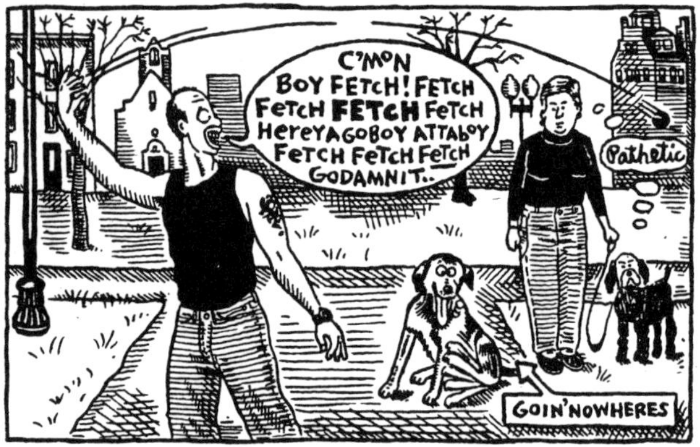
C'MON BOY FETCH! FETCH FETCH FETCH FETCH HEREYAGOBOY ATTABOY FETCH FETCH FETCH GODAMNIT..
Pathetic
GOIN'NOWHERES

POOPED TWICE WHEN EETH ONLY BROUGHT 1 BAG.

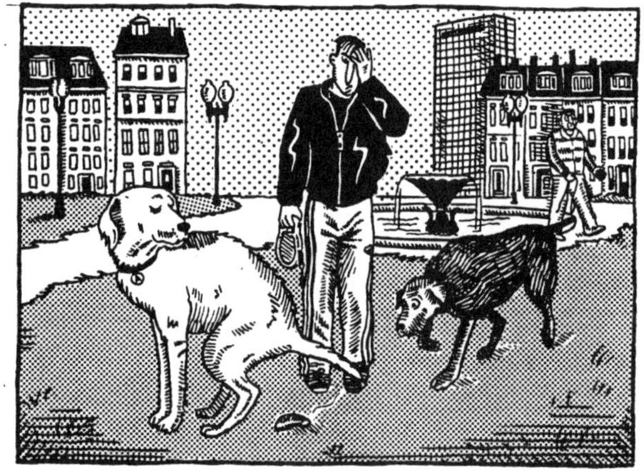

ATE GARBAGE SHE FOUND ON CURB..

MAKES BEELINE ACROSS PARK TO JUMP ON GUY WEARING NICE SUIT..

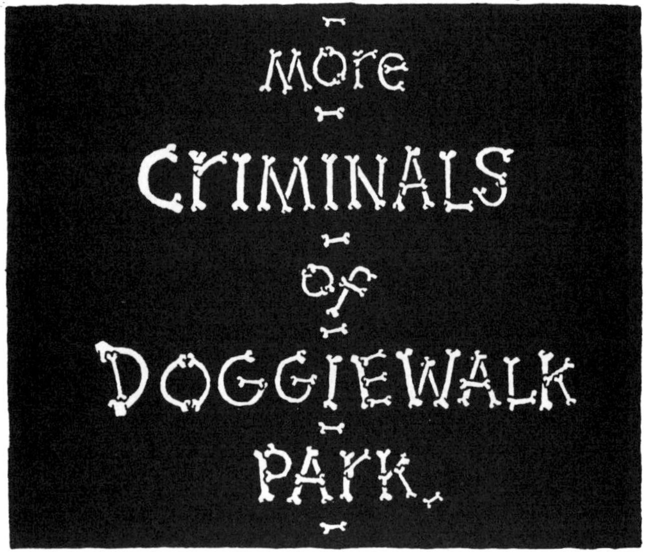
more
CRIMINALS
of
DOGGIEWALK
PARK.

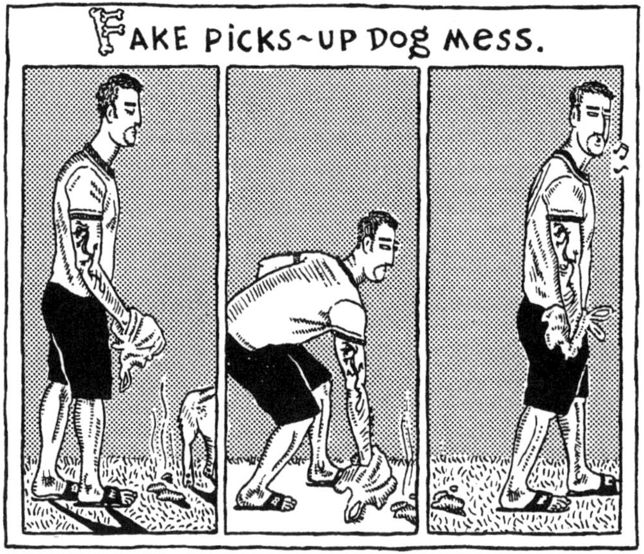
FAKE PICKS~UP DOG MESS.

Eats bread crumbs put out by nice Korean lady for pigeons.

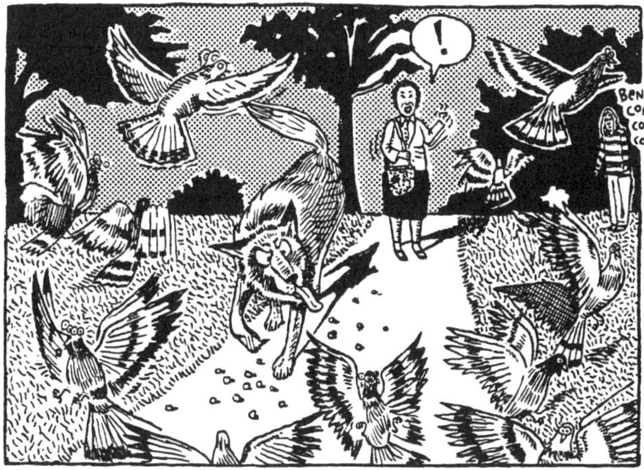
!
Benny come. come come

Thinks toddlers are weird, uppity dogs wearing clothing, & barks at them accordingly..

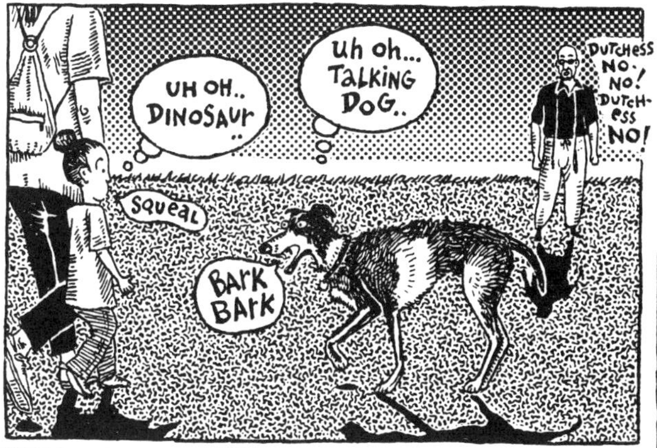
Uh oh.. Dinosaur..
Uh oh... Talking dog..
Dutchess no. no! Dutch-ess no!
Squeal
Bark Bark

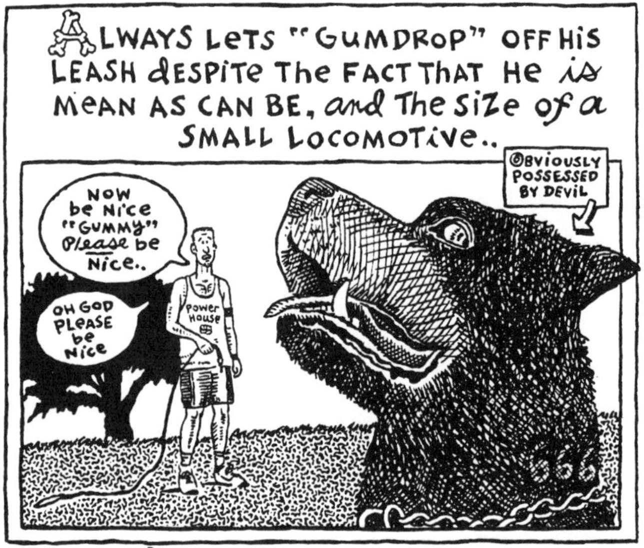
ALWAYS LETS "GUMDROP" OFF HIS LEASH despite The FACT THAT He is mean AS CAN BE, and The size of a SMALL LOCOMOTive..
OBVIOUSLY POSSESSED BY DEVIL
NOW be Nice "GUMMY" Please be Nice..
OH GOD PLEASE be Nice
Power House
666

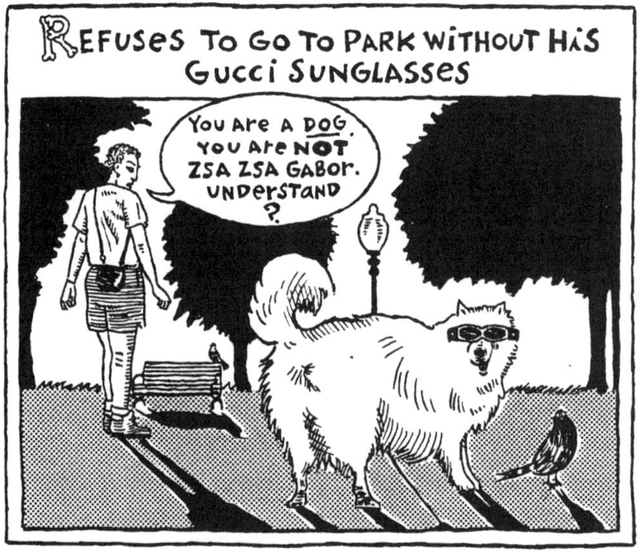
REFUSES TO GO TO PARK WITHOUT HIS GUCCI SUNGLASSES
You Are A DOG. You Are NOT ZSA ZSA GABOR. UNDERSTAND ?

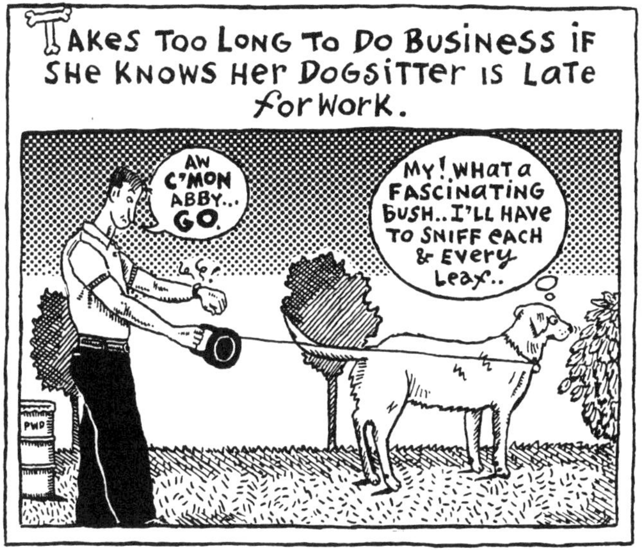
TAKES TOO LONG TO DO BUSINESS IF SHE KNOWS HER DOGSITTER IS LATE FOR WORK.
AW C'MON ABBY... GO.
MY! WHAT A FASCINATING BUSH.. I'LL HAVE TO SNIFF EACH & EVERY LEAF..
PWD

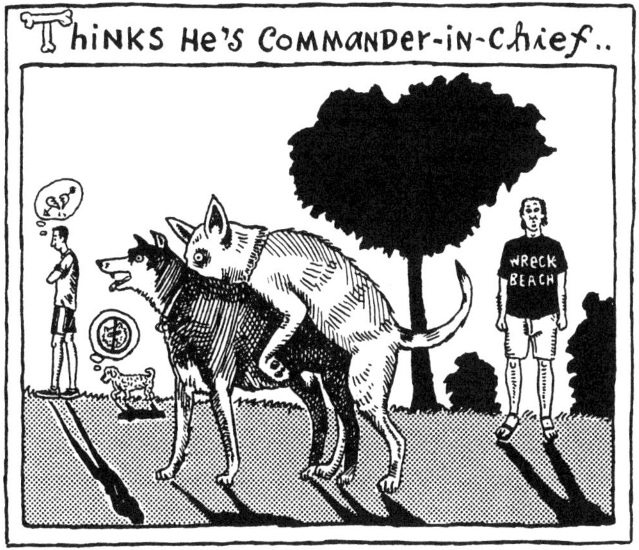
THINKS HE'S COMMANDER-IN-CHIEF..
WRECK BEACH

ODD MAN IN

So a year ago I get invited to this brunch. It's the Queen Mother's Birthday, or Solstice, some holiday they never celebrated on Grant street.

I don't really know anyone there, except the hosts and they're busy keeping the guests in Mimosas. This guy comes onto me pretty strong. He's hot and I'm horny — and lonely — so I ask him if he wants to leave.

It's sunny at my place and there's a nice cross breeze and we have sex and lay there smoking a joint, and he tells me his lover is in Texas for the week.

I should've been pissed but I'm not even surprised. This guy's too unguarded to be single. And I could've asked...

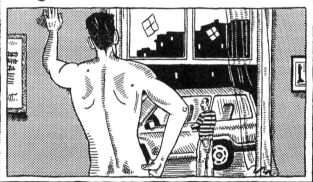

The next week I call him at work. He says why don't I have dinner with him and Carlos. That Carlos is cooking molé, which can be kind of heavy but come anyway.

We smoke pot again, and Carlos is charming and funny. They're both charming and funny. And I stay the night and I am dead on my feet the next day at the hospital.

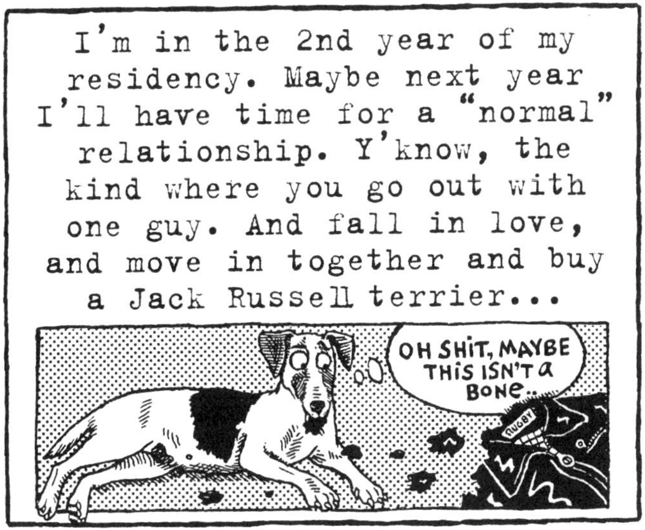
I'm in the 2nd year of my residency. Maybe next year I'll have time for a "normal" relationship. Y'know, the kind where you go out with one guy. And fall in love, and move in together and buy a Jack Russell terrier...
OH SHIT, MAYBE THIS ISN'T a BONE..

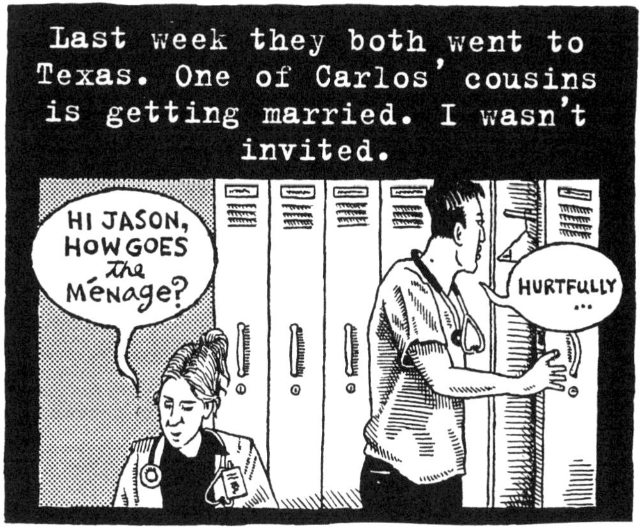
Last week they both went to Texas. One of Carlos' cousins is getting married. I wasn't invited.
HI JASON, HOW GOES the MÉNAGE?
HURTFULLY...

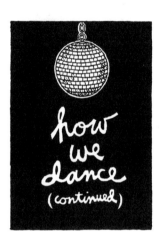

how we dance
(continued)

Santa Agua: The Saint Bernard of dance floors. Spends the evening ferrying bottled water to & fro.

CARLOS, JASON, STAY HYDRATED!

WHAT DID HE JUST SAY?

"CARLOS, JASON, THE CLUB'S BEING RAIDED"

OH..

The Wandering Jew: In a chronic state of having lost his girlfriends the minute he crosses a club's threshold.

HAVE YOU SEEN BUCKY?

OK, IF YOU SEE BUCKY WILL YOU TELL HIM I'M LOOKING FOR HIM UPSTAIRS...

OK, HAVE YOU SEEN TODD?

HOW ABOUT JASON CHANG?

AT THE BAR?

WHICH BAR?

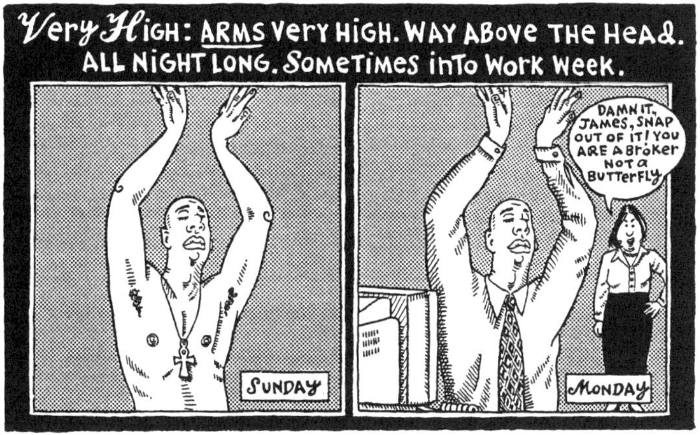
Very High: ARMS very HIGH. WAY ABove THE HEAD. ALL NIGHT LONG. SomeTIMES into Work Week.
DAMN IT, JAMES, SNAP OUT OF IT! YOU ARE A Broker NOT a BUTTERFLY.
SUNDAY
MONDAY

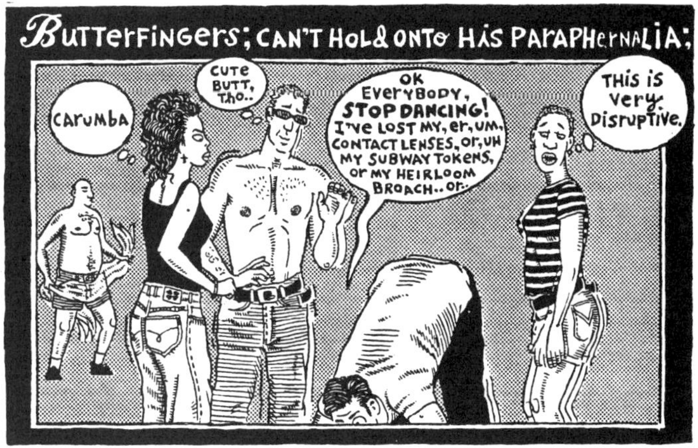
Butterfingers; CAN'T HOLD ONTO HIS PARAPHERNALIA;
CARUMBA
CUTE BUTT, Tho..
OK EVERYBODY, STOP DANCING! I've LOST MY, er, UM, CONTACT LENSES, or, UH MY SUBWAY TOKENS, or MY HEIRLOOM BROACH.. or..
THIS is very. DISRUPTIVE.

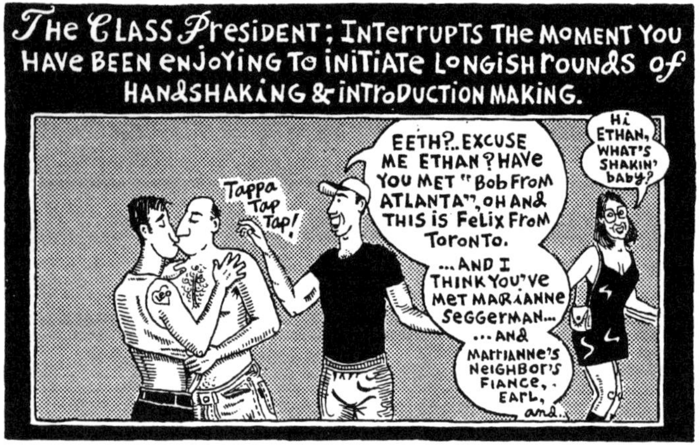
The Class President; Interrupts the moment you have been enjoying to initiate longish rounds of handshaking & introduction making.
Tappa Tap Tap!
EETH?.. EXCUSE ME ETHAN? HAVE YOU MET "Bob From ATLANTA", OH AND THIS is Felix From Toronto.
... AND I THINK YOU'VE MET MARIANNE SEGGERMAN...
... AND MARRIANNE'S NEIGHBOR'S FIANCE, . EARL, and..
Hi ETHAN, WHAT'S SHAKIN' baby?

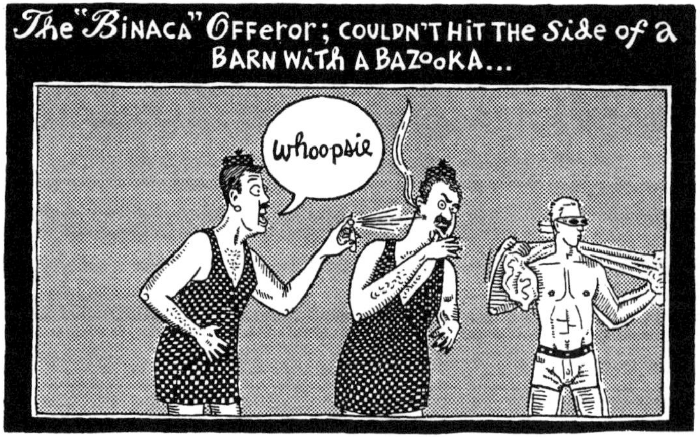
The "Binaca" Offeror; couldn't hit the side of a barn with a bazooka...
whoopsie

THE ETHAN GREEN *Guide to* GREETINGS

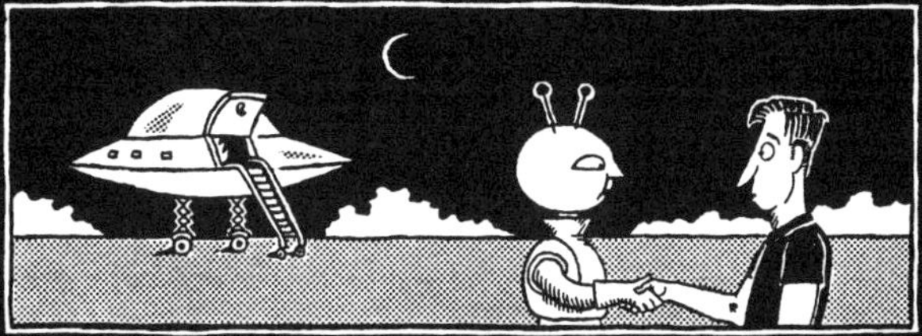

THE CHEEK TOSSER

Is he protecting you from catching his cold? Or does he just find you gross as can be? You'll probably never know.

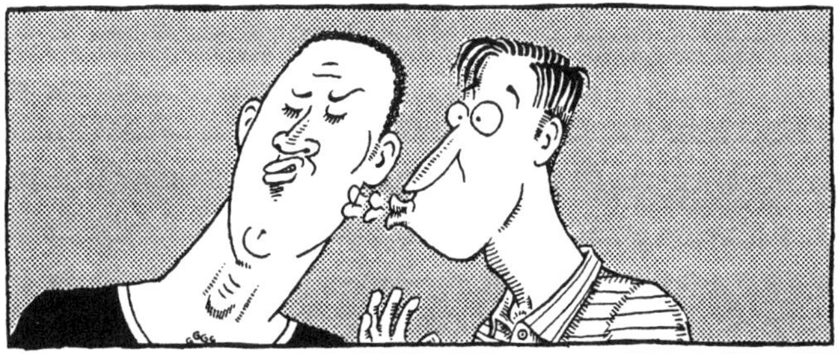

THE GROUPER

Wet. Wide Open. And comin' right at you. Scary.

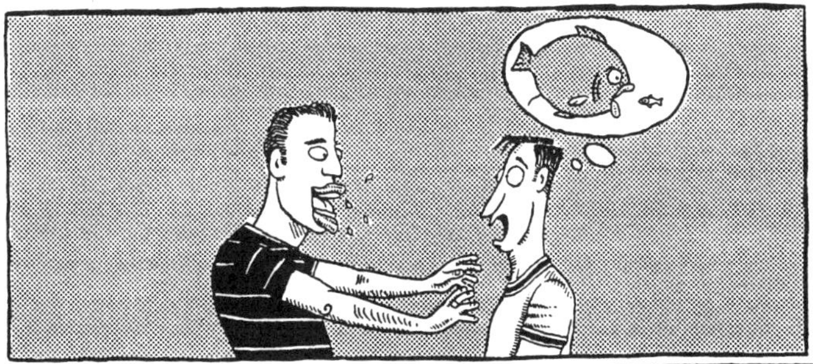

THE LINGERER

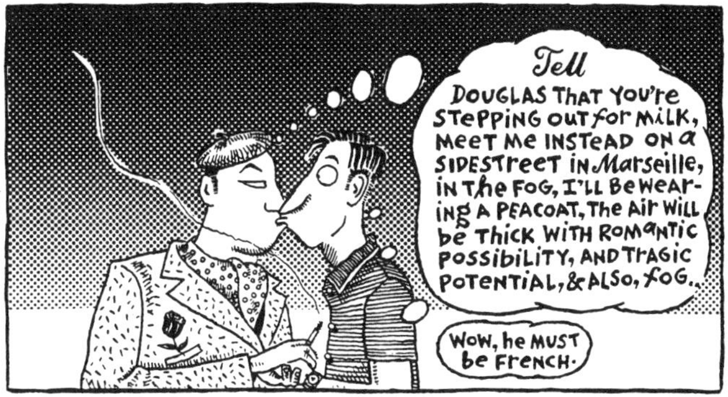
Tell DOUGLAS THAT YOU'RE STEPPING OUT FOR MILK, MEET ME INSTEAD ON A SIDESTREET IN Marseille, IN THE FOG, I'LL BE WEARING A PEACOAT, THE AIR WILL BE THICK WITH ROMANTIC POSSIBILITY, AND TRAGIC POTENTIAL, & ALSO, FOG..
WOW, HE MUST BE FRENCH.

Whoopsie #1
(Air smooch in a straight setting)

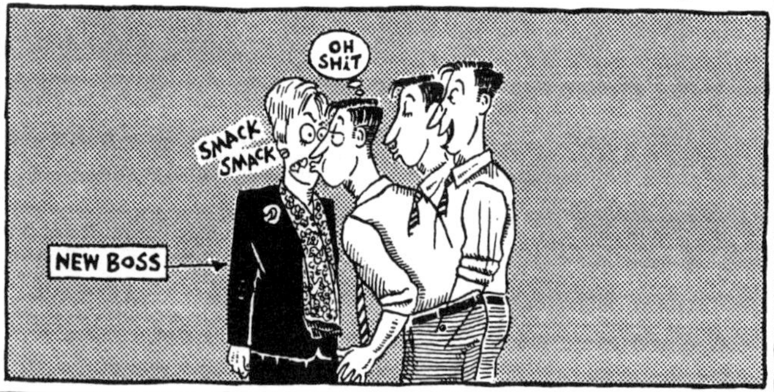
OH SHIT
SMACK SMACK
NEW BOSS

Whoopsie #2
(Handshake in a queer setting)

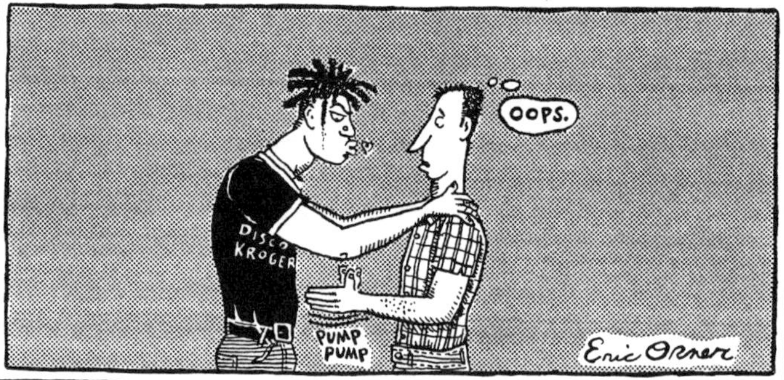
OOPS.
DISCO KROGER
PUMP PUMP
Eric Orner

todd's
Bitterness primer for today
1 Files suit regularly against ex boyfriends.
YOUR HONOR, WE COLLECTED THOSE JADE FIGURINES TOGETHER! BUT 58% OF THEM ARE AT HIS PLACE!
NOT TO MENTION ALL THE CALPHALON
..OR THE KOHLER BATHROOM FIXTURES..
2 is countersued just as regularly.
I'VE GOT TO GET OFF the FAG DRAMA DOCKET.
WELL HE ALLOWED ME TO PAY FOR HIS ENTIRE graduate SCHOOL EDUCATION while CHEATING ON ME WITH A SUCCESSION OF STUDENT ADVISORS, LECTURERS & TEACHING ASSISTANTS.. truly..
oh puhlease.
LIKE I WOULD SLEEP WITH a T.A.
TODD'S EQUALLY NOXIOUS & SMARMY ex, "RODD"

③ FORBIDS MOM FROM SENDING EX BIRTHDAY GREETING.

④ fINDS OUT THE SNEAKY OLD WITCH (TODD'S TERM, NOT MINE) SENT IT ANYWAY...

OH, TODD, HI.. YOUR MOM SENT ME THE *sweetest* CARD! I WAS SO TOUCHED! TRULY..

HATE HIM CAN'T BELIEVE I DATED HIM.

PRIAPE

WE'RE DOING LUNCH AND A MATINEE NEXT THURSDAY.. I JUST LUV HER. *Truly*

68

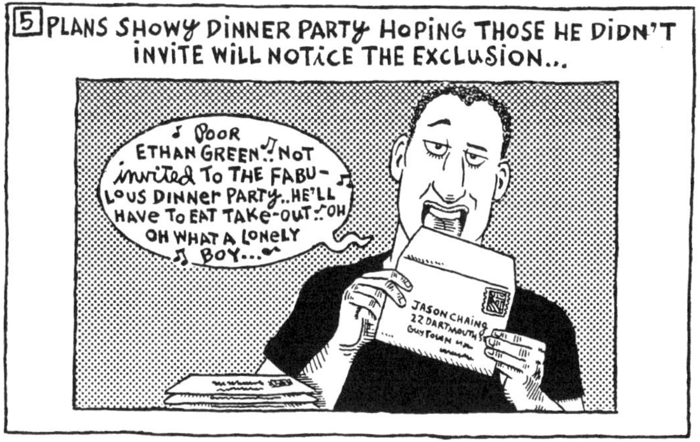
5 PLANS SHOWY DINNER PARTY HOPING THOSE HE DIDN'T INVITE WILL NOTICE THE EXCLUSION...
♪ Poor ETHAN GREEN ♪ NOT invited TO THE FABU-LOUS DINNER PARTY.. HE'LL HAVE TO EAT TAKE-OUT ♪ OH OH WHAT A LONELY ♪ BOY...

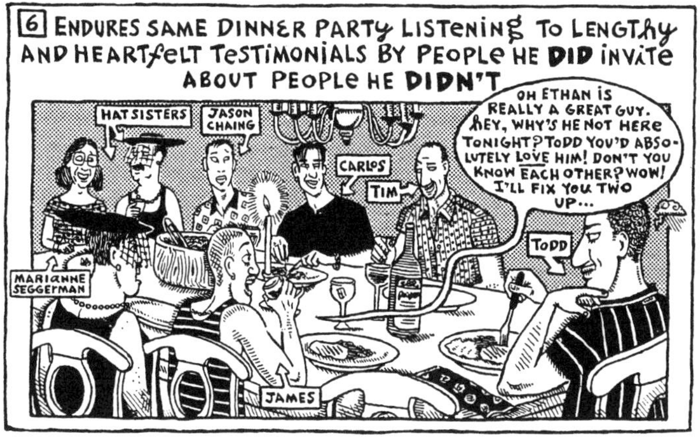
6 ENDURES SAME DINNER PARTY LISTENING TO LENGTHY AND HEARTFELT TESTIMONIALS BY PEOPLE HE **DID** INVITE ABOUT PEOPLE HE **DIDN'T**
HAT SISTERS
JASON CHAING
CARLOS
TIM
OH ETHAN IS REALLY A GREAT GUY. HEY, WHY'S HE NOT HERE TONIGHT? TODD YOU'D ABSOLUTELY LOVE HIM! DON'T YOU KNOW EACH OTHER? WOW! I'LL FIX YOU TWO UP...
TODD
MARIANNE SEGGERMAN
JAMES

Fishing for Answers...
The Guys Consider Our Hero's Current State of Marital disarray
..SO, NO SOONER HAVE THESE "PROMISEKEEPERS" MADE THEIR SOLEMN VOWS TO BE BETTER HUSBANDS & DADS, THEN THEY'RE OFF ON A GUYS-ONLY-WEEKEND-ROAD-TRIP TO DC.. I GUESS GOD WILL MOW THE LAWN AND TAKE THE KIDS TO THE MALL.
Oh... I TOLD DOUG I WANT US TO LIVE TO-GETHER..

WHAT? I'M NOT MOVING IN WITH YOU.. I MEAN, NO OFFENSE, BUT...
SEEING WHOLE LIFE FLASH BEFORE HIS EYES.
THAT'S ME AND DOUG, NOT ME AND YOU, PROFESSOR HAWKING, Sheesh...
OH! WHYDINCH'A SAY SO! CONGRATS..
SO?.. HOW'D HE REACT? DID HE GET ALL WIGGED OUT?
Y'KNOW IF YOU DO THAT LONG ENOUGH, YOUR FACE'LL FREEZE THAT WAY AND WE'LL HAVE TO SEND YOU OFF TO A SANATARIUM.. I'VE GOT PRACTICE, LATER...
empty vase "flowers"
HI EETH..
HEY MOON.
"ALL WIGGED OUT" (A DEMONSTRATION)

DON'T BE LATE! WE'RE HAVING Risotto, IT RUINS IF YOU'RE LATE!
bye
YOU'RE LIKE THIS SOCCER MOM NOW, AREN'T YOU?
LIKE THIS WHAT?
forget it..
SO? WHAT HAPPENED AFTER YOU TOLD him YOU WANT TO LIVE TOGETHER?
HE WENT ON A 2 WEEK FISHING TRIP WITH HIS DAD...
WOW... YOU REALLY FREAKED HIM OUT.
bigTIME
I'M NOT SURE WHAT WOULD GET ME IN A TENT WITH MY DAD FOR TWO WEEKS.. SOME CRAZED RUSSIAN MOBSTER WITH A STOLEN NUKE THREATENING TO BLOW UP SAN FRANCISCO, MAYBE.. OR PTOWN... even SOUTH BEACH...
(SIGH) WHAT AM I GONNA DO?
ABOUT THE MOBSTER?
ABOUT DOUG..
Meanwhile..
(SIGH) WHAT AM I GONNA DO?
ABOUT ETHAN...
ABOUT THAT WALLEYE?

Le Village Revisité

So you are moping at home after an argument with Doug about moving in together, when, a voice you hadn't expected to hear surprises you.

Apparently the Mounties have let Etienne out of prison.

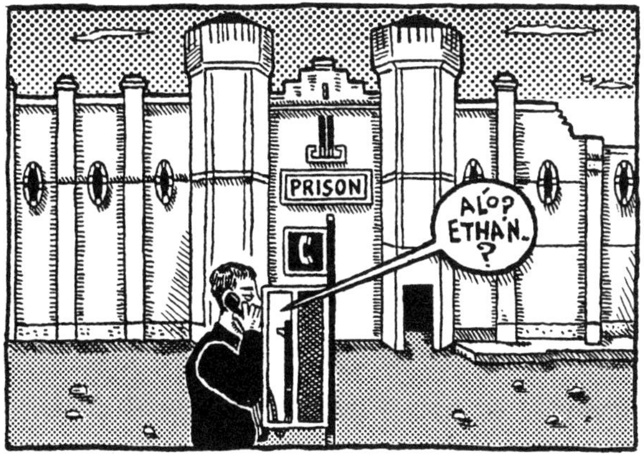
PRISON
ALÓ? ETHAN..?

He admits to having behaved unpleasantly last year, and offers to make it up to you by inviting you to the reopening of his Outremont bistro.

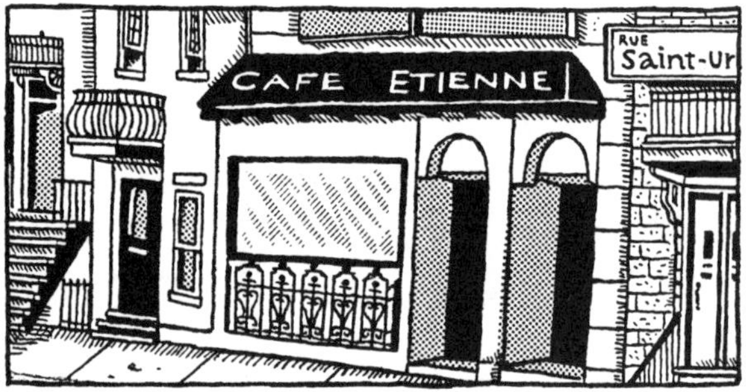
CAFE ETIENNE
RUE Saint-Ur

Well, Doug's on a fishing trip with his dad, and it's not like you've gotta datebook full of engagements for the weekend. God knows you love Montréal. What the hell, you accept.

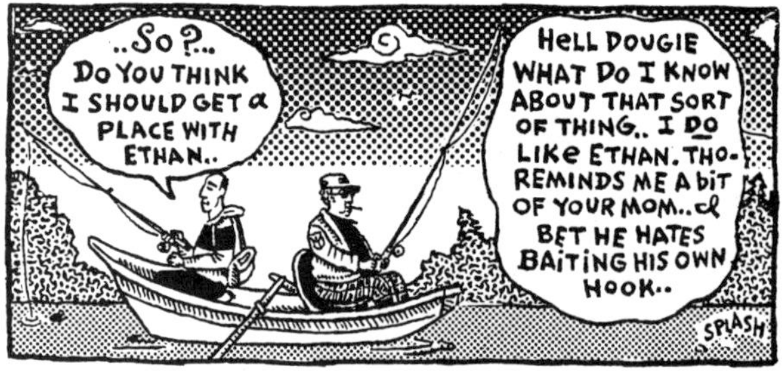
..So?.. DO YOU THINK I SHOULD GET a PLACE WITH ETHAN..
HELL DOUGIE WHAT DO I KNOW ABOUT THAT SORT OF THING.. I DO LIKE ETHAN. THO- REMINDS ME A BIT OF YOUR MOM..I'd BET HE HATES BAITING HIS OWN HOOK..
SPLASH

You aren't sleeping with him. You're not even attracted to him anymore, which allows you to relax and enjoy his company.

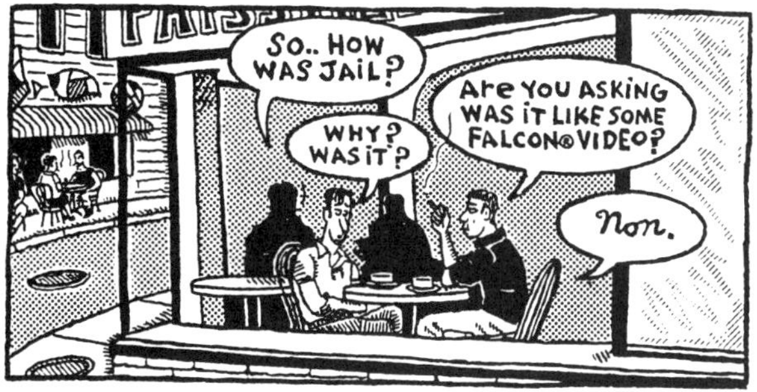
SO.. HOW WAS JAIL?
WHY? WAS IT?
ARE YOU ASKING WAS IT LIKE SOME FALCON® VIDEO?
Non.

The opening is nice. Marvelous food, musicians, painters, people with day jobs who "write". A guy on the balcony talking up separation.

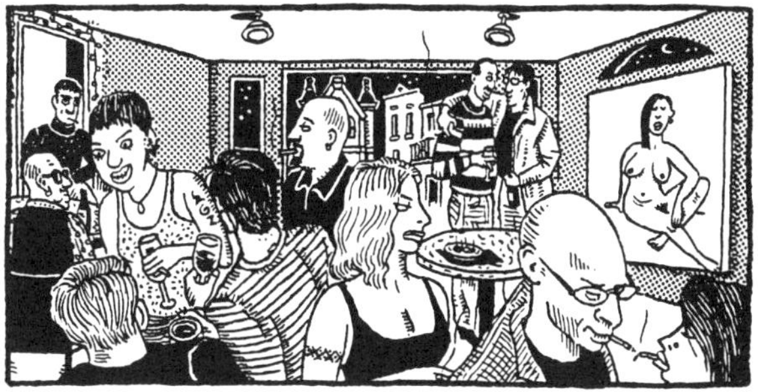

Leeza, his faghag, is all-of-a-
sudden your best pal. She says
she's going to be in "your neck
of the woods next month".
You're a little drunk, and offer
to put her up when she comes.

She and he certainly are
conspiratorial. It's nice that
you couldn't care less what
about, anymore...

Later..

DID HE AGREE TO LET YOU STAY WITH HIM?

OF COURSE.

EXCELLENT EXCELLENT.

To be Continued

76

Really Pretty Far Off the Circuit Circuit Parties

with your host, Ethan Green

FUR AND ICE PARTY
Yellowknife, North West Territories

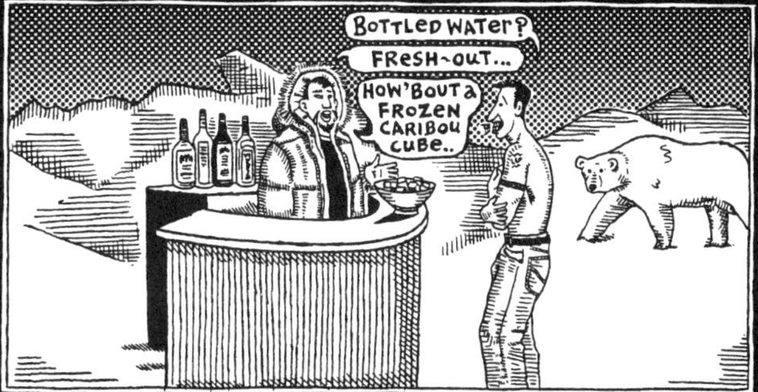
BOTTLED WATER?
FRESH-OUT...
HOW'BOUT a FROZEN CARIBOU CUBE..

HUMIDITY-RUINED-HER-HAIR PARTY
Amarillo

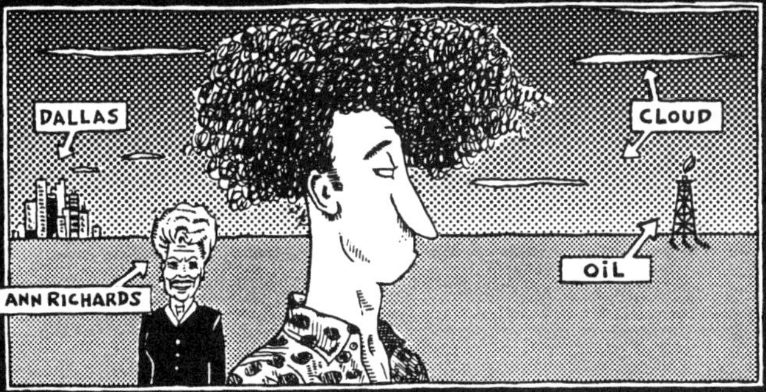
DALLAS
CLOUD
OIL
ANN RICHARDS

CORN COB PARTY
Des Moines (famed for its floor shows)

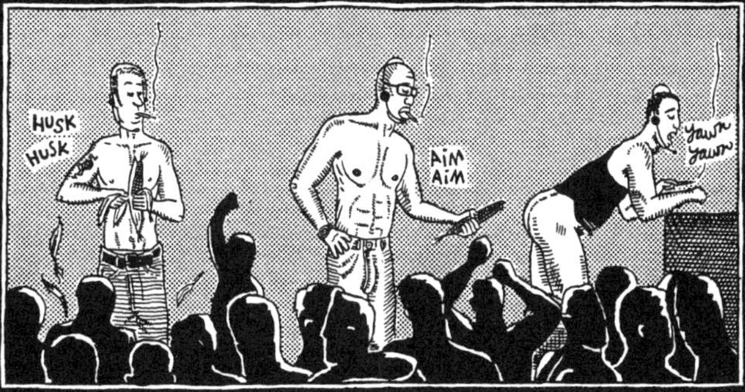
HUSK
HUSK
AIM
AIM
yawn
yawn

DRIZZLE AND MOOR PARTY
Glasgow

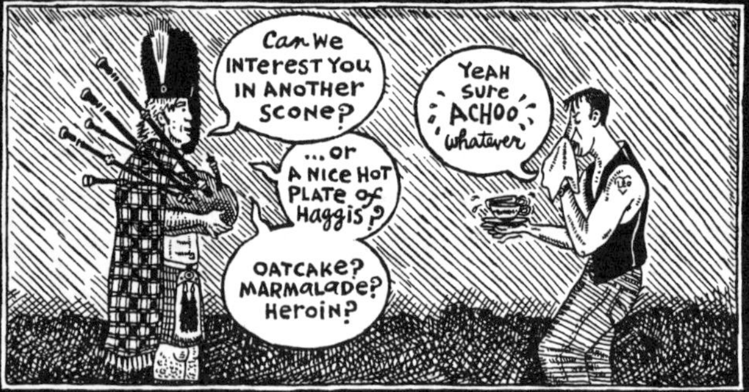
Can we INTERest You IN ANOTHer SCONe?
...or A NICe HOT PLATe of Haggis?
OATCAKe? MARMaLaDe? HeroIN?
YeAH Sure ACHOO whatever

BLACK PARTY
Sioux Falls

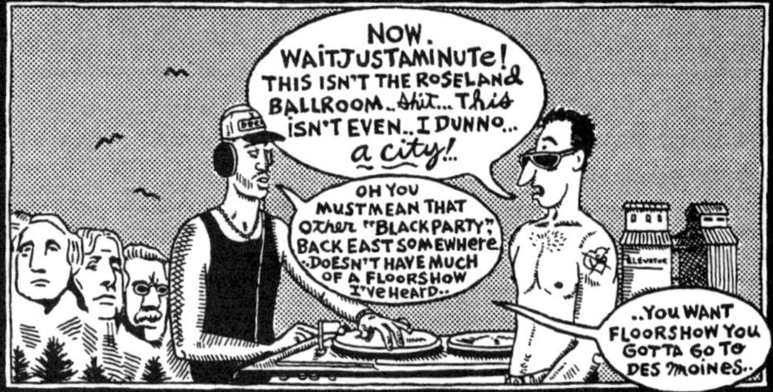
NOW. WAITJUSTAMINUTe! THIS ISN'T THE ROSELAND BALLROOM.. ~~shit~~... This ISN'T EVEN.. I DUNNO... a city!..
OH YOU MUSTMEAN THAT other "BLACKPARTY", BACK EAST SOMEWHere ..DOESN'T HAVE MUCH OF A FLOORSHOW I'Ve HeARD..
..YOU WANT FLOORSHOW YOU GOTTA GO TO DES Moines..

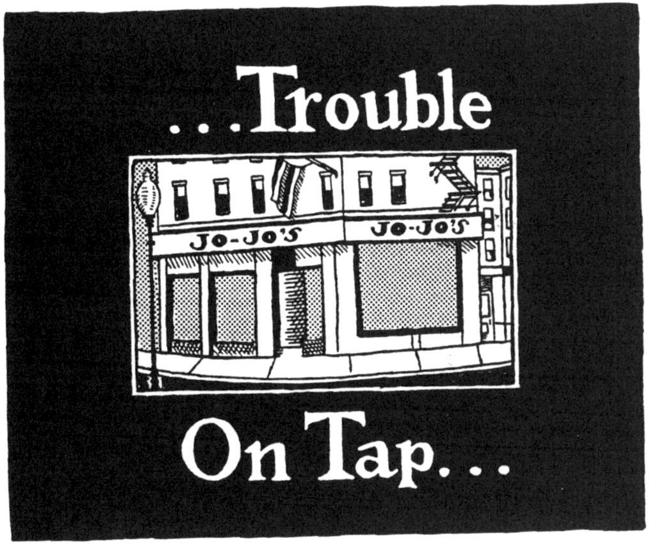

...Trouble
JO-JO'S
JO-JO'S
On Tap...

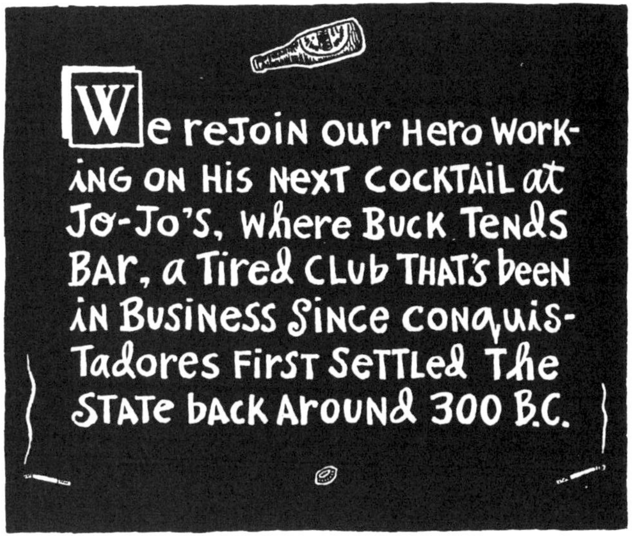

We rejoin our Hero working on his next cocktail at Jo-Jo's, where Buck tends bar, a tired club that's been in business since conquistadores first settled the state back around 300 B.C.

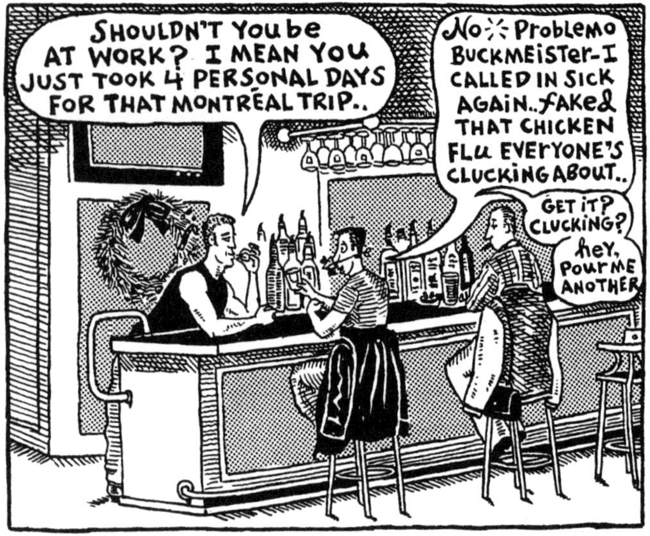
SHOULDN'T YOU BE AT WORK? I MEAN YOU JUST TOOK 4 PERSONAL DAYS FOR THAT MONTRÉAL TRIP..
NO PROBLEMO BUCKMEISTER- I CALLED IN SICK AGAIN.. FAKED THAT CHICKEN FLU EVERYONE'S CLUCKING ABOUT..
GET IT? CLUCKING?
HEY, POUR ME ANOTHER

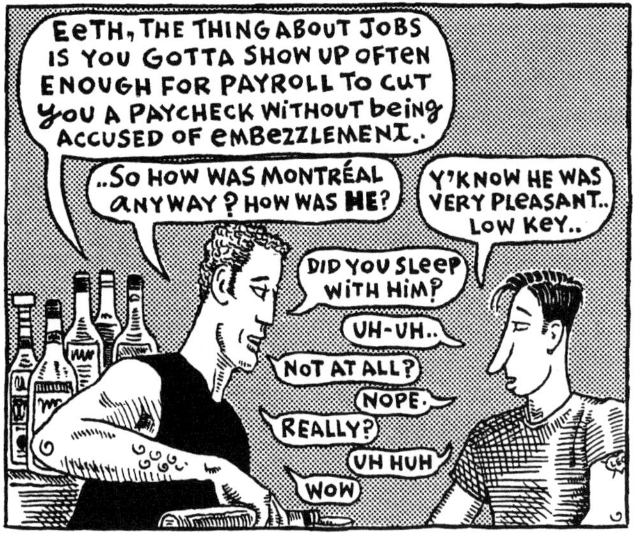
EETH, THE THING ABOUT JOBS IS YOU GOTTA SHOW UP OFTEN ENOUGH FOR PAYROLL TO CUT YOU A PAYCHECK WITHOUT BEING ACCUSED OF EMBEZZLEMENT..
..SO HOW WAS MONTRÉAL ANYWAY? HOW WAS **HE**?
Y'KNOW HE WAS VERY PLEASANT.. LOW KEY..
DID YOU SLEEP WITH HIM?
UH-UH..
NOT AT ALL?
NOPE.
REALLY?
UH HUH
WOW

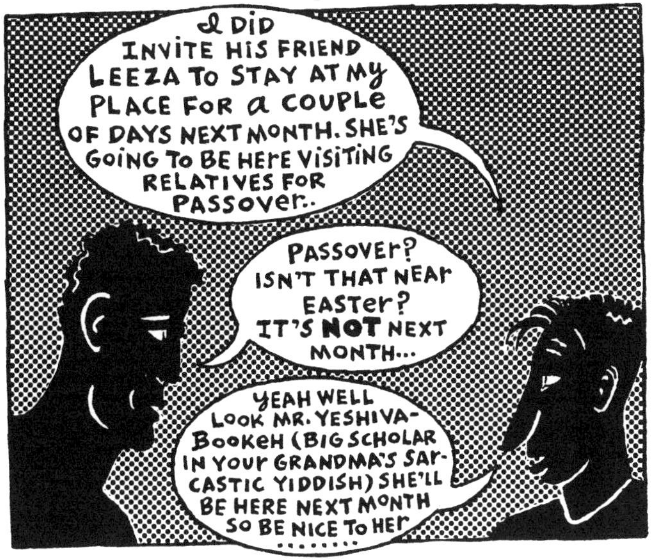
I DID INVITE HIS FRIEND LEEZA TO STAY AT MY PLACE FOR A COUPLE OF DAYS NEXT MONTH. SHE'S GOING TO BE HERE VISITING RELATIVES FOR PASSOVER..
PASSOVER? ISN'T THAT NEAR EASTER? IT'S **NOT** NEXT MONTH...
YEAH WELL LOOK MR. YESHIVA-BOOKEH (BIG SCHOLAR IN YOUR GRANDMA'S SARCASTIC YIDDISH) SHE'LL BE HERE NEXT MONTH SO BE NICE TO HER ....

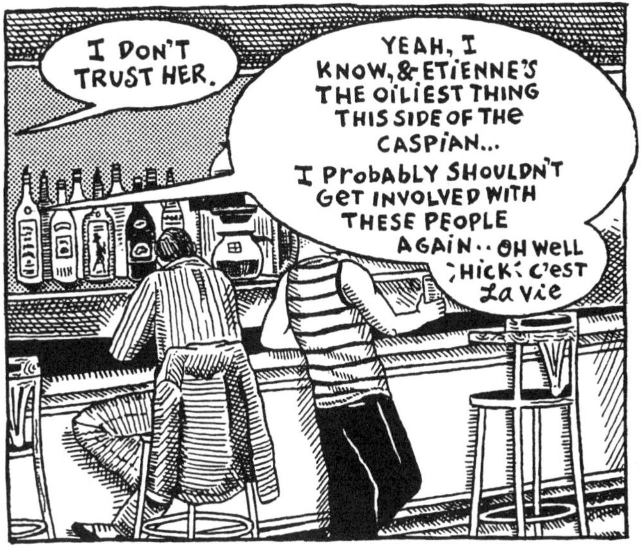
I DON'T TRUST HER.
YEAH, I KNOW, & ETIENNE'S THE OILIEST THING THIS SIDE OF THE CASPIAN... I PROBABLY SHOULDN'T GET INVOLVED WITH THESE PEOPLE AGAIN.. OH WELL ;HICK; C'EST LA VIE

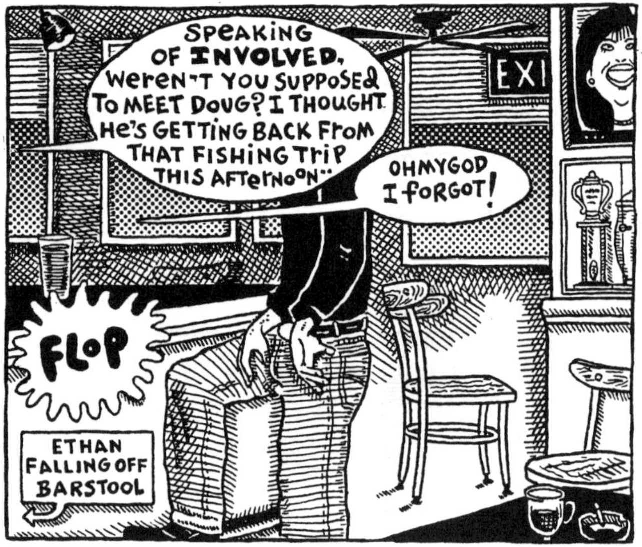
SPEAKING OF INVOLVED, WEREN'T YOU SUPPOSED TO MEET DOUG? I THOUGHT HE'S GETTING BACK FROM THAT FISHING TRIP THIS AFTERNOON..
OHMYGOD I FORGOT!
FLOP
ETHAN FALLING OFF BARSTOOL
EXI
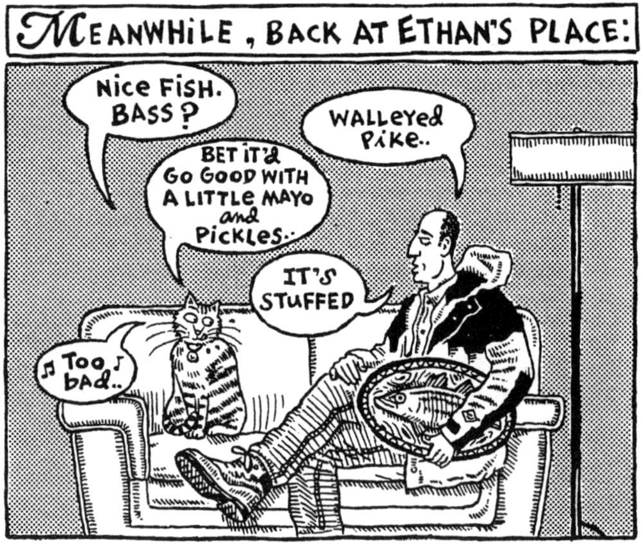
MEANWHILE, BACK AT ETHAN'S PLACE:
NICE FISH. BASS?
WALLEYED PIKE..
BET IT'D GO GOOD WITH A LITTLE MAYO AND PICKLES..
IT'S STUFFED
♫ TOO BAD.. ♫

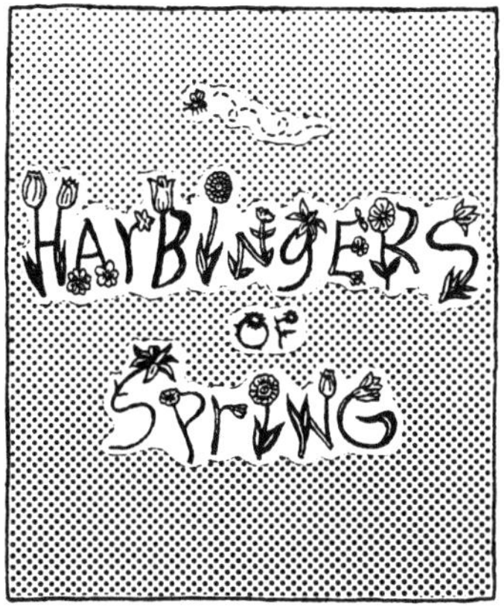
HARBINGERS OF SPRING

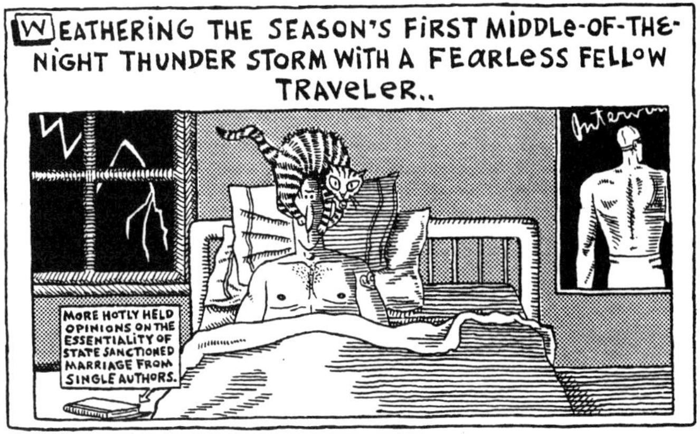
WEATHERING THE SEASON'S FIRST MIDDLE-OF-THE-NIGHT THUNDER STORM WITH A FEARLESS FELLOW TRAVELER..
MORE HOTLY HELD OPINIONS ON THE ESSENTIALITY OF STATE SANCTIONED MARRIAGE FROM SINGLE AUTHORS.

THE SWELL OF DOUG'S beautiful CALVES bunched UP AGAINST THE TOP OF his ROLLERBLADES.

WALKING TO BRUNCH OOHING AND AAHING OVER THE first CROCUSES & DAFFODILS.

WOW.

—SIGH—

big WHUP.

HUSH MOON, YOUR AUNT ETHAN & I ARE HAVING A MOMENT.

SIDEWALK CRUISING, SUCCESSFULLY...
...AND UNSUCCESSFULLY.
CLONK

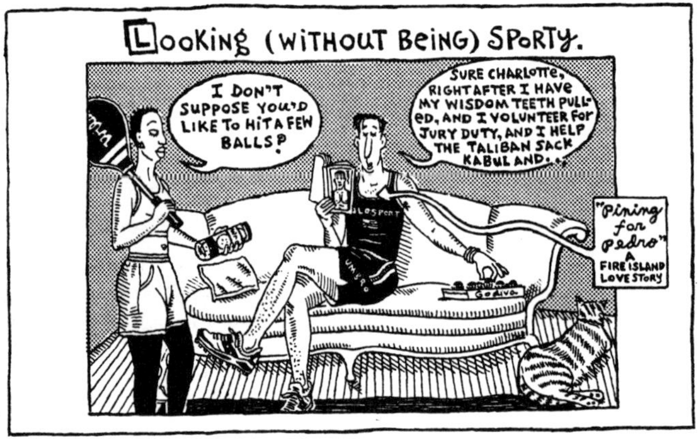
LOOKING (WITHOUT BEING) SPORTY.
I DON'T SUPPOSE YOU'D LIKE TO HIT A FEW BALLS?
SURE CHARLOTTE, RIGHT AFTER I HAVE MY WISDOM TEETH PULLED, AND I VOLUNTEER FOR JURY DUTY, AND I HELP THE TALIBAN SACK KABUL AND...
"Pining for Pedro" A FIRE ISLAND LOVE STORY
Godiva

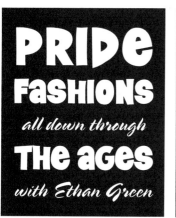

PRIDE FASHIONS

all down through

THE AGES

with Ethan Green

1985
Pre-Rainbow

LAMBDA EARRING

DAUGHTERS OF BILITIS SUN VISOR

PINK TRIANGLE

AWKWARD SLOGAN-EERING

GO GAY

FRIENDSHIP BRACELET

1989
Dawning of Rainbow Awareness
(Kind of the bronze age of rainbow accesorization)

TORTOISE SHELL JFK-STYLE RAYBANS

RAINBOW-COLORED FREEDOM RINGS

MY OTHER GIRLFRIEND IS A GUY

MORE AWKWARD SLOGANEERING

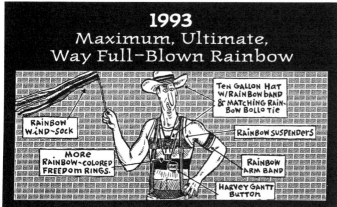

1993
Maximum, Ultimate, Way Full-Blown Rainbow

TEN GALLON HAT W/RAINBOW BAND & MATCHING RAINBOW BOLLO TIE

RAINBOW WIND-SOCK

RAINBOW SUSPENDERS

MORE RAINBOW-COLORED FREEDOM RINGS

RAINBOW ARM BAND

HARVEY GANTT BUTTON

1995
Rainbow-So-Last-Week
(Over the Rainbow)

NON RAINBOW CAP

NON RAINBOW SHIRT

DON'T ASK DON'T TELL DON'T WORK BUTTON

AMERICAN FLAG PIN WITH RAINBOW STRIPES

NON RAINBOW (ALLCHROME) FREEDOM RINGS

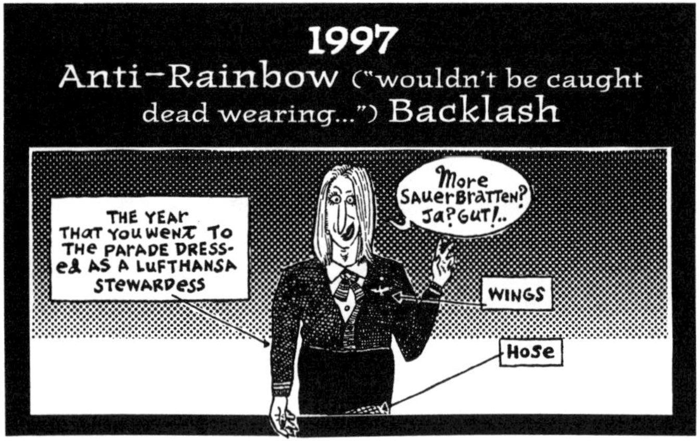
1997
Anti-Rainbow ("wouldn't be caught dead wearing...") Backlash
THE YEAR THAT YOU WENT TO THE PARADE DRESSED AS A LUFTHANSA STEWARDESS
More SAUERBRATTEN? Ja? GUT!..
WINGS
HOSE

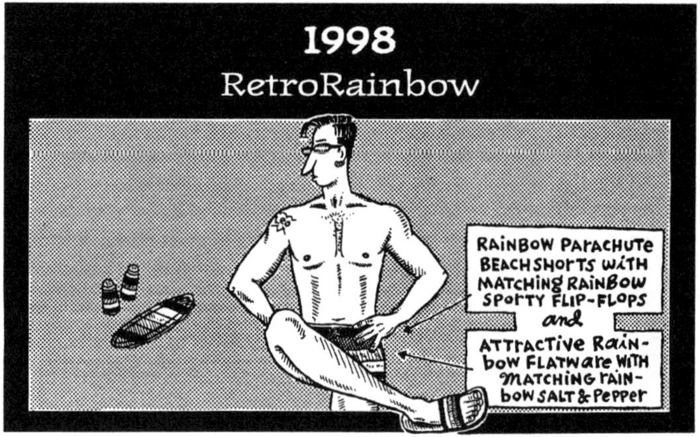
1998
RetroRainbow
RAINBOW PARACHUTE BEACH SHORTS WITH MATCHING RAINBOW SPORTY FLIP-FLOPS
and
ATTRACTIVE RAIN-bow FLATWARE WITH MATCHING RAIN-bow SALT & Pepper

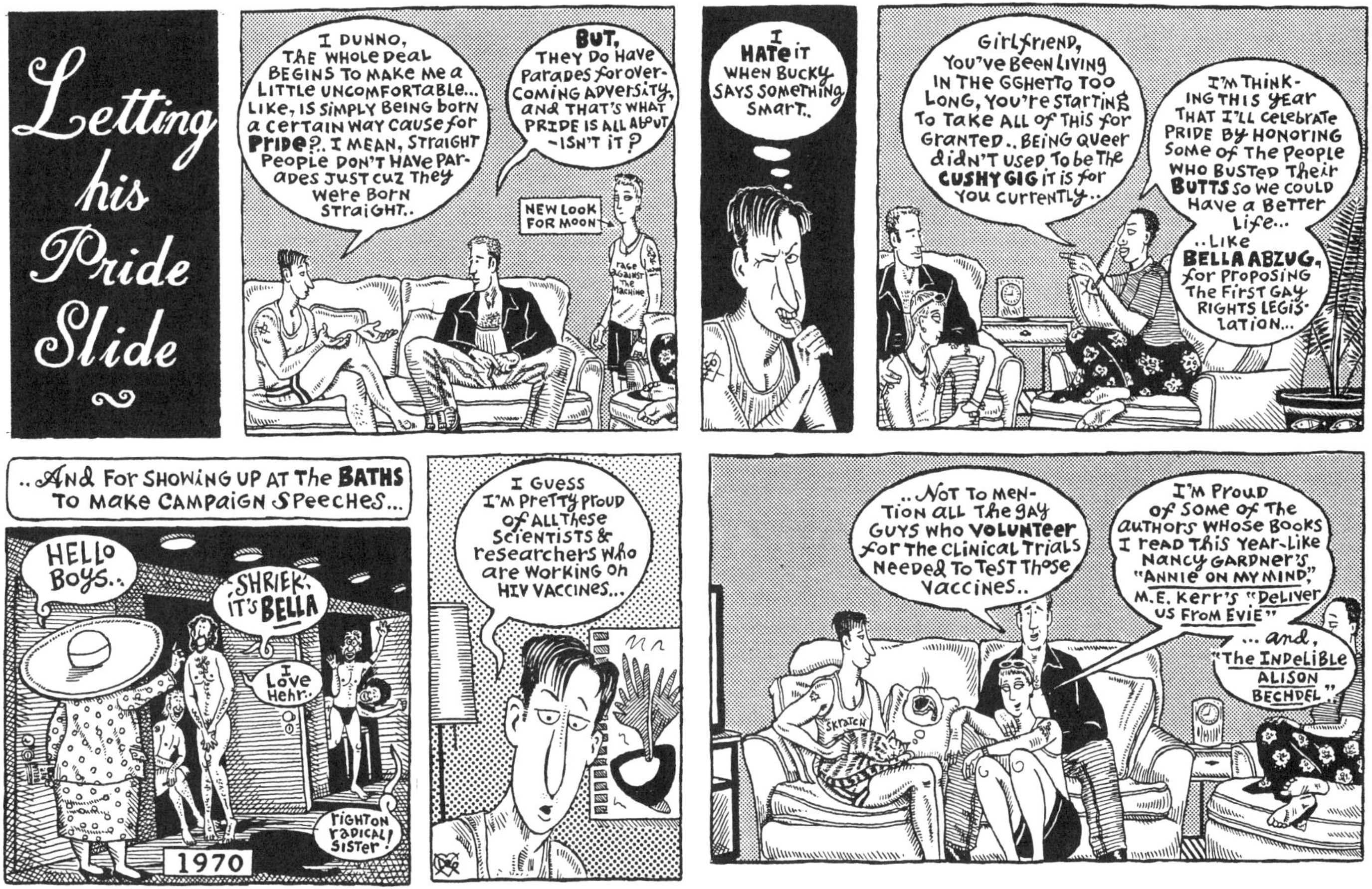
Letting his Pride Slide
I dunno, the whole deal begins to make me a little uncomfortable... like, is simply being born a certain way cause for PRIDE?.. I mean, straight people don't have parades just cuz they were born straight..
BUT, they do have parades for overcoming adversity, and that's what pride is all about -isn't it?
NEW LOOK FOR MOON
Rage against the machine
I HATE it when Bucky says something smart..
Girlfriend, you've been living in the gghetto too long, you're starting to take all of this for granted.. being queer didn't used to be the CUSHY GIG it is for you currently..
I'm thinking this year that I'll celebrate pride by honoring some of the people who busted their BUTTS so we could have a better life...
..like BELLA ABZUG, for proposing the first gay rights legislation...
..And for showing up at the BATHS to make campaign speeches...
Hello boys..
Shriek it's BELLA
I love hehr.
Right on radical sister!
1970
I guess I'm pretty proud of all these scientists & researchers who are working on HIV vaccines...
..Not to mention all the gay guys who VOLUNTEER for the clinical trials needed to test those vaccines..
I'm proud of some of the authors whose books I read this year-like Nancy Gardner's "Annie on my mind," M.E. Kerr's "Deliver us from Evie"
...and, "The Indelible Alison Bechdel".
Skratch

...So, How'r you doing now, Betty Blasé, crisis of confidence all blown over? Feeling good about ourselves again?
yeah,.. THANKS, CharL'...
My Pleasure
WOW, you read ALL THOSE?
..WELL The Last one's mostly a cartoon book..
Oh Pleeze, Do We HAVE To HAVE one of These Embarassing faux paternal moments..
KISS

Another day,
Another
Dollar...
9:06 AM. YOU'RE LATE. NO MUSIC ON RADIO, JUST MORNING-JOCK IDIOCY.
HEY THERE MORNING CREW!! BE DOO BE DOO..
DOO? EEEU!
HA HA! YES! THAT WUZ HOOTIE...
ONE WAY
10:00 AM. YOU WRESTLE WITH THE "LOCKING" MECHANISM ON YOUR COFFEE'S LID... IT WINS.
...YOU NEED A FRIGGING PHD IN ENGINEERING TO WORK THESE THINGS!!
MONTY
POOLE

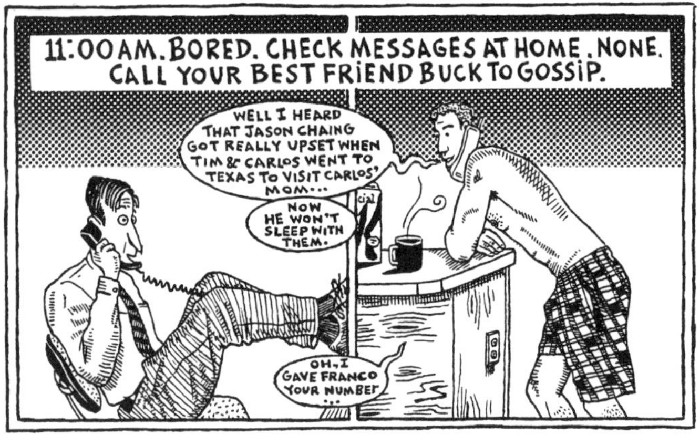
11:00 AM. BORED. CHECK MESSAGES AT HOME. NONE. CALL YOUR BEST FRIEND BUCK TO GOSSIP.
WELL I HEARD THAT JASON CHAING GOT REALLY UPSET WHEN TIM & CARLOS WENT TO TEXAS TO VISIT CARLOS' MOM...
NOW HE WON'T SLEEP WITH THEM.
OH, I GAVE FRANCO YOUR NUMBER...

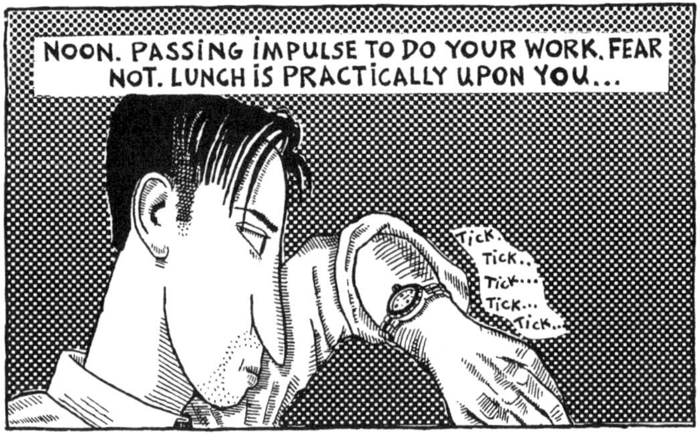
NOON. PASSING IMPULSE TO DO YOUR WORK. FEAR NOT. LUNCH IS PRACTICALLY UPON YOU...
TICK..
TICK..
TICK...
TICK...
TICK..

2:00PM. POST-LUNCH BLOOD SUGAR CRASH. CHECK MESSAGES AGAIN, IN DESPARATE BID TO NOT FALL ASLEEP AT DESK...

YEA THIS'S FRANCO, THE GUY YOU WUZ CRUISIN' LAST WEEK WHEN YOU WALKED INTO THAT SIGN. A LITTLE DORKY, BUT CUTE... CALL ME...

HERE'S MY BEEPER NUMBER:

NELLIE DELA

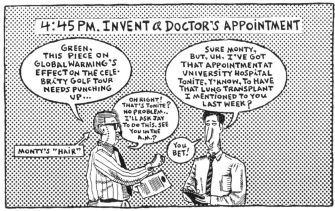

4:45 PM. INVENT a DOCTOR'S APPOINTMENT

GREEN, THIS PIECE ON GLOBAL WARMING'S EFFECT ON THE CELE-BRITY GOLF TOUR NEEDS PUNCHING UP...

OH RIGHT! THAT'S TONITE? NO PROBLEM.. I'LL ASK JAY TO DO THIS. SEE YOU IN THE A.M.?

MONTY'S "HAIR"

SURE MONTY, BUT, UH, I'VE GOT THAT APPOINTMENT AT UNIVERSITY HOSPITAL TONITE, Y'KNOW, TO HAVE THAT LUNG TRANSPLANT I MENTIONED TO YOU LAST WEEK?

YOU BET!

93

Rejection Ain't Pretty

Thursday

DALLAS

Friday

Tuesday

MANY OF THE ANCIENT CULTURES OF ANTIQUITY CONSIDERED *an* UNRINGING PHONE TO BE INDICATIVE OF A VISIT FROM THE REJECTION GODDESS...

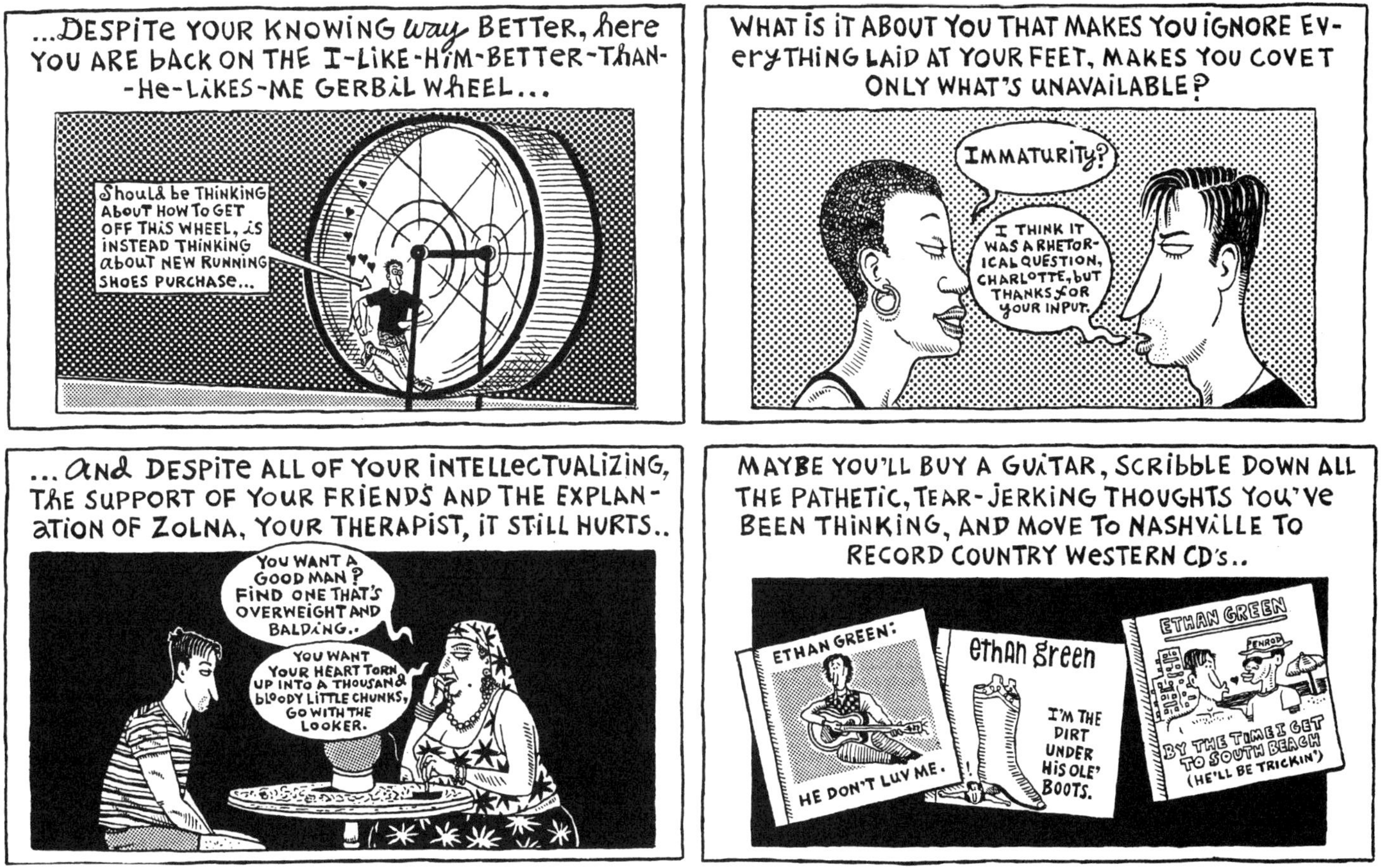
...DESPITE YOUR KNOWING way BETTER, here YOU ARE BACK ON THE I-LIKE-HIM-BETTER-THAN-HE-LIKES-ME GERBIL WHEEL...
Should be THINKING ABOUT HOW TO GET OFF THIS WHEEL, IS INSTEAD THINKING ABOUT NEW RUNNING SHOES PURCHASE...
WHAT IS IT ABOUT YOU THAT MAKES YOU IGNORE EVERYTHING LAID AT YOUR FEET, MAKES YOU COVET ONLY WHAT'S UNAVAILABLE?
IMMATURITY?
I THINK IT WAS A RHETORICAL QUESTION, CHARLOTTE, BUT THANKS FOR YOUR INPUT.
...AND DESPITE ALL OF YOUR INTELLECTUALIZING, THE SUPPORT OF YOUR FRIENDS AND THE EXPLANATION OF ZOLNA, YOUR THERAPIST, IT STILL HURTS..
YOU WANT A GOOD MAN? FIND ONE THAT'S OVERWEIGHT AND BALDING..
YOU WANT YOUR HEART TORN UP INTO A THOUSAND BLOODY LITTLE CHUNKS, GO WITH THE LOOKER.
MAYBE YOU'LL BUY A GUITAR, SCRIBBLE DOWN ALL THE PATHETIC, TEAR-JERKING THOUGHTS YOU'VE BEEN THINKING, AND MOVE TO NASHVILLE TO RECORD COUNTRY WESTERN CD's..
ETHAN GREEN:
HE DON'T LUV ME.
ethan green
I'M THE DIRT UNDER HIS OLE' BOOTS.
ETHAN GREEN
PENROD
BY THE TIME I GET TO SOUTH BEACH
(HE'LL BE TRICKIN')

On the off chance that you are re-thinking those monastic vows you made after that last guy broke your heart, the Ethan Green Public Service Dept Presents this...

Dream Date

alphabet

Arturo is Attitude-y

SNIFF

Bill is a Bitch

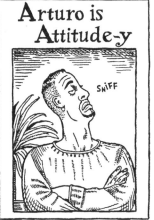

THOSE JEANS MAKE HIS BUTT LOOK ENORMOUS.

Chad is Cheap

SO, THAT COMES TO LEMME SEE, I'D SAY ABOUT $10 FOR YOU & $3.75 FOR ME, UM YOU KNOW, 'CUZ YOU HAD THAT EXTRA PEPSI..

BEEP BEEP BEEP

Denton is Drugged

POLO SPORT

..and Ephrahaim is an Ego-maniac.

YOU MEAN TO SAY I'VE NEVER SHOWN YOU MY SCRAPBOOK? WELL PULL UP A CHAIR YOU'RE IN FOR A TREAT!

LOOK HERE'S ME AT JUNIOR BOWLING

Fernando is Fake

O.M.G!

GIRLF

GIRLF

96

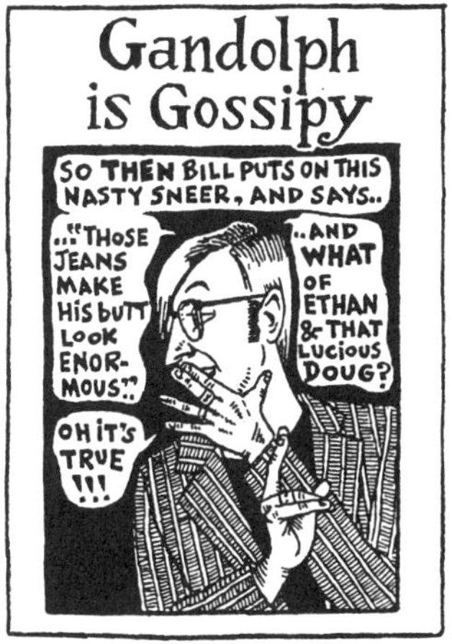
Gandolph is Gossipy
SO THEN BILL PUTS ON THIS NASTY SNEER, AND SAYS..
..."THOSE JEANS MAKE HIS BUTT LOOK ENORMOUS."
..AND WHAT OF ETHAN & THAT LUCIOUS DOUG?
OH IT'S TRUE !!!

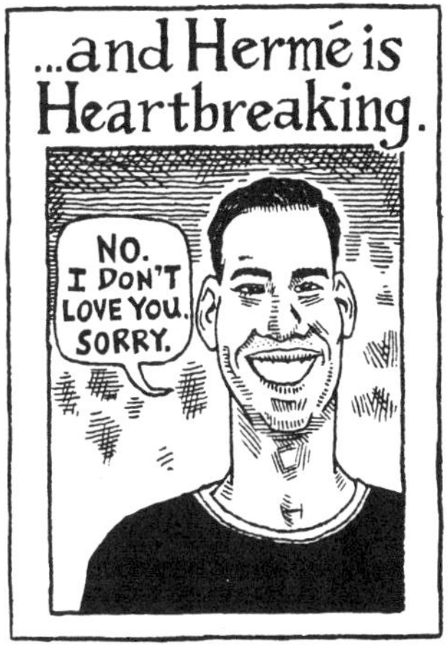
...and Hermé is Heartbreaking.
NO. I DON'T LOVE YOU. SORRY.

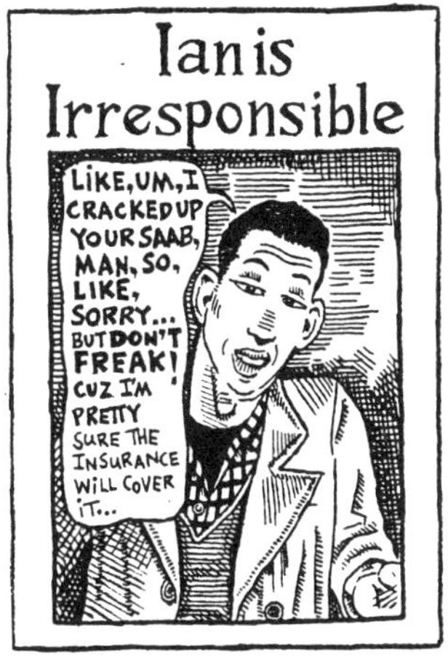
Ian is Irresponsible
LIKE, UM, I CRACKED UP YOUR SAAB, MAN, SO, LIKE, SORRY... BUT DON'T FREAK! CUZ I'M PRETTY SURE THE INSURANCE WILL COVER IT...

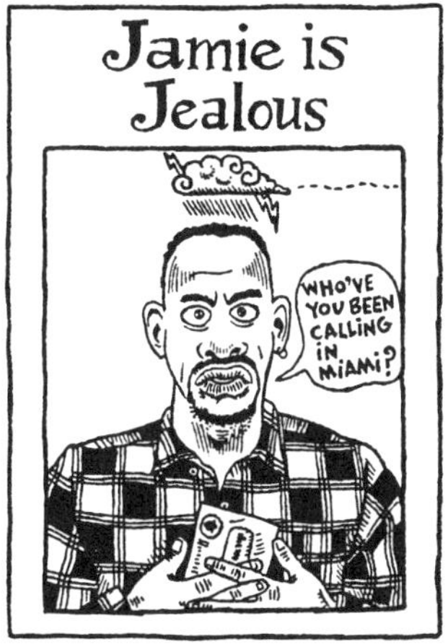
Jamie is Jealous
WHO'VE YOU BEEN CALLING IN MIAMI?

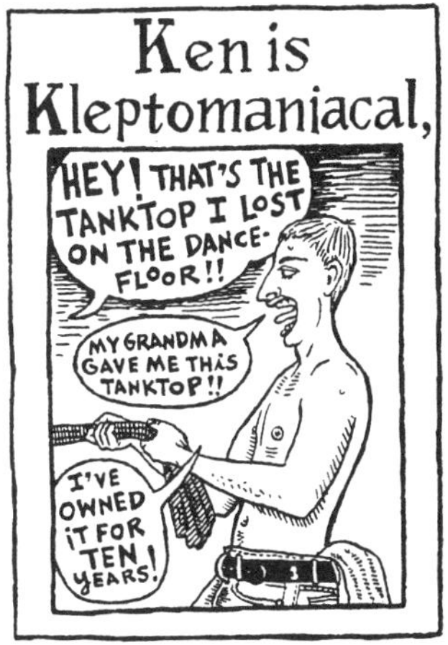
Ken is Kleptomaniacal,
HEY! THAT'S THE TANKTOP I LOST ON THE DANCE-FLOOR!!
MY GRANDMA GAVE ME THIS TANKTOP!!
I'VE OWNED IT FOR TEN YEARS!

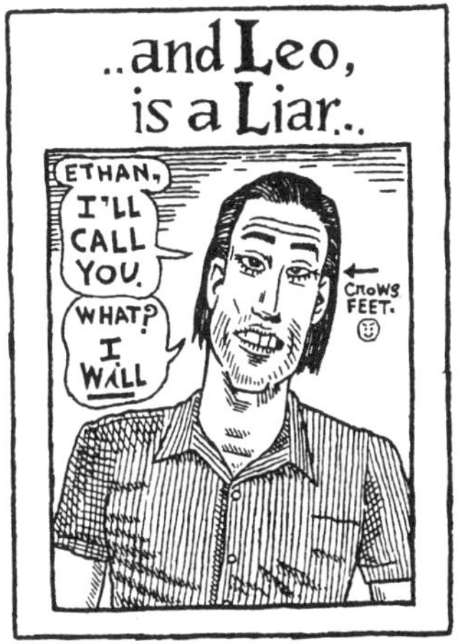
..and Leo, is a Liar..
ETHAN, I'LL CALL YOU.
WHAT?
I WILL
CROWS FEET.

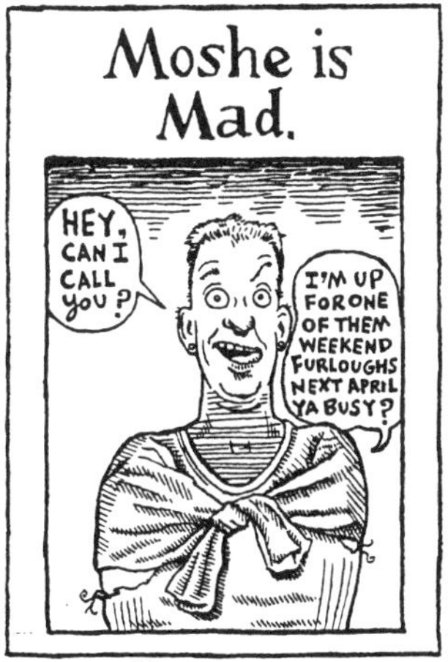
Moshe is Mad.
HEY, CAN I CALL YOU?
I'M UP FOR ONE OF THEM WEEKEND FURLOUGHS NEXT APRIL YA BUSY?

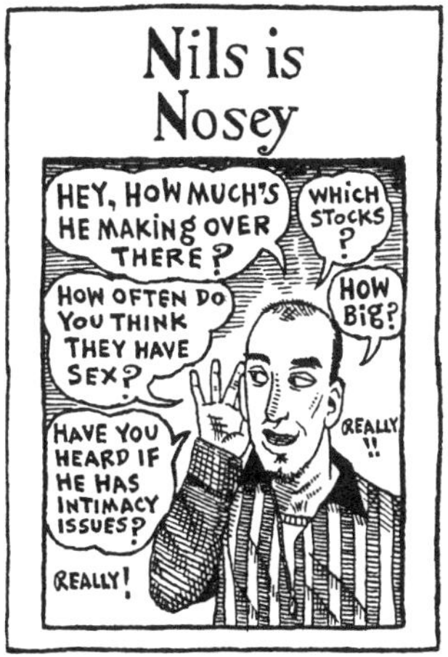
Nils is Nosey
HEY, HOW MUCH'S HE MAKING OVER THERE?
WHICH STOCKS?
HOW BIG?
HOW OFTEN DO YOU THINK THEY HAVE SEX?
HAVE YOU HEARD IF HE HAS INTIMACY ISSUES?
REALLY!!
REALLY!

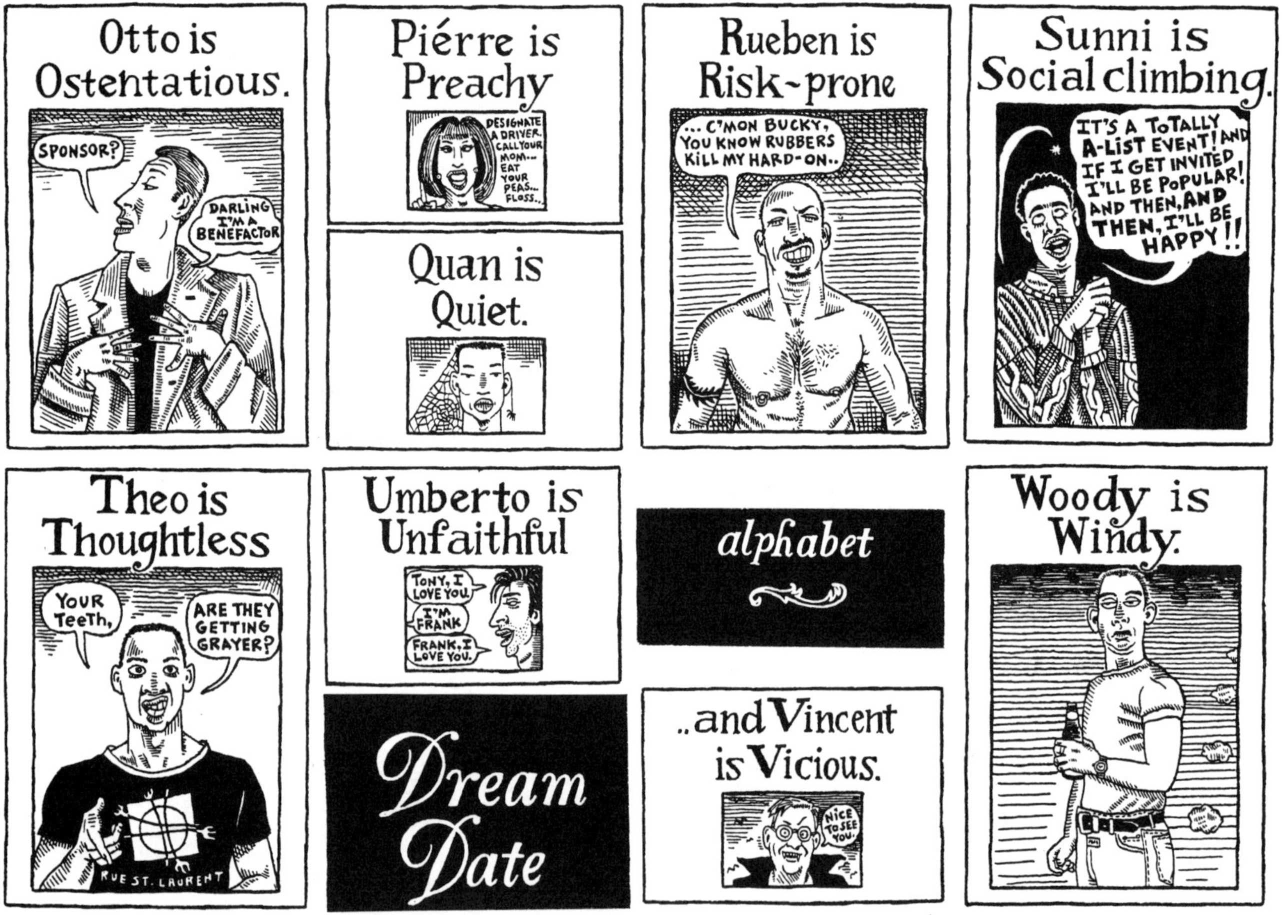
Otto is Ostentatious.
SPONSOR?
DARLING I'M A BENEFACTOR
Piérre is Preachy
DESIGNATE A DRIVER. CALL YOUR MOM... EAT YOUR PEAS... FLOSS..
Quan is Quiet.
Rueben is Risk-prone
... C'MON BUCKY, YOU KNOW RUBBERS KILL MY HARD-ON..
Sunni is Social climbing.
IT'S A TOTALLY A-LIST EVENT! AND IF I GET INVITED I'LL BE POPULAR! AND THEN, AND THEN, I'LL BE HAPPY!!
Theo is Thoughtless
YOUR TEETH,
ARE THEY GETTING GRAYER?
RUE ST. LAURENT
Umberto is Unfaithful
TONY, I LOVE YOU.
I'M FRANK
FRANK, I LOVE YOU.
Dream Date
alphabet
..and Vincent is Vicious.
NICE TO SEE YOU.
Woody is Windy.

Xerces is Xenophobic
Jersey-ites OUT OF PHILLY
Yaegel is Young...
I'M a TOP.
REAL MEN ARE TOPS.
...and Zack is Zombiesque.
GOTTA EAT THIS BONE
GOTTA EAT THIS BONE
GOTTA EAT THIS BONE
GOTTA EAT THIS BONE

How to ruin a perfectly nice Sunday afternoon.

With your hosts, Ethan & Doug

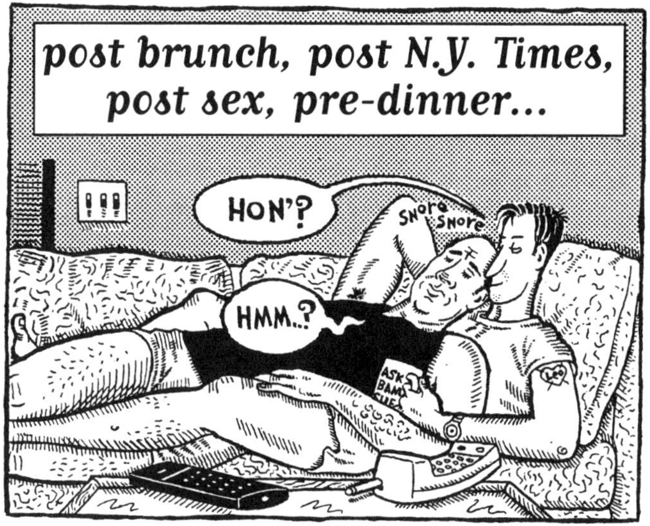
post brunch, post N.Y. Times, post sex, pre-dinner...
HON'?
SNore SNore
HMM.?

D'YOU WANT TO MEET BUCK & CHARL' AND HAVE CHINESE FOR DINNER?
MMM.. YEA THAT'D BE NICE.. COUPLE OF HOURZZZZZ
HON?
MMM?

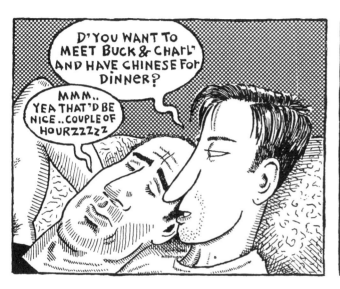

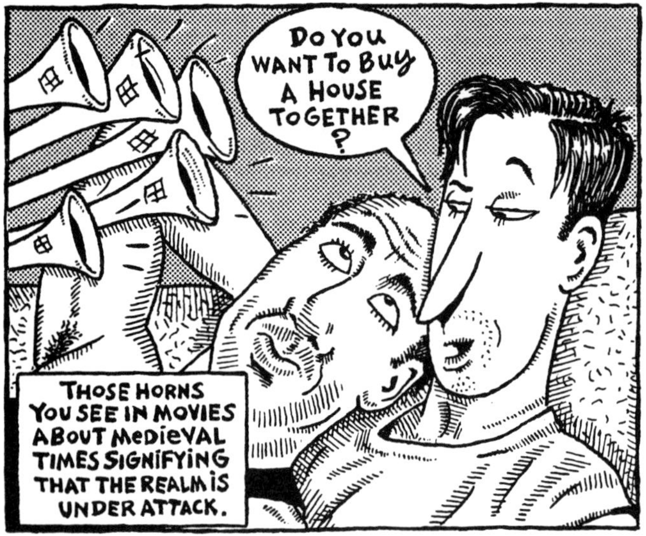
DO YOU WANT TO BUY A HOUSE TOGETHER ?
THOSE HORNS YOU SEE IN MOVIES ABOUT MEDIEVAL TIMES SIGNIFYING THAT THE REALM IS UNDER ATTACK.

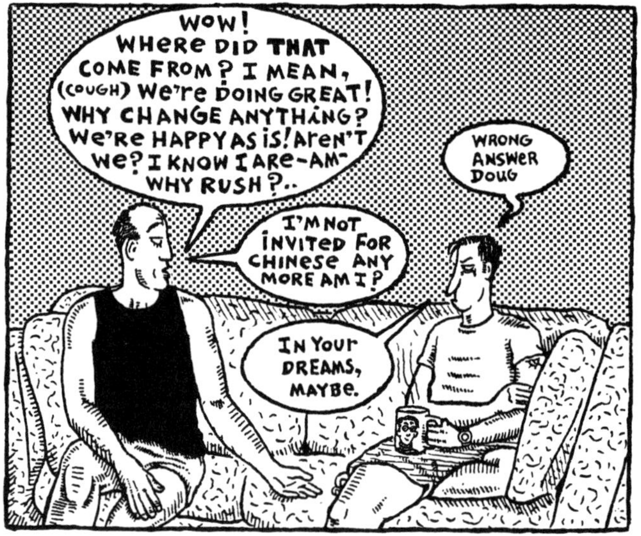
WOW! WHERE DID THAT COME FROM? I MEAN, (COUGH) WE'RE DOING GREAT! WHY CHANGE ANYTHING? WE'RE HAPPY AS IS! AREN'T WE? I KNOW I ARE-AM- WHY RUSH?..
WRONG ANSWER DOUG
I'M NOT INVITED FOR CHINESE ANY MORE AM I?
IN YOUR DREAMS, MAYBE.

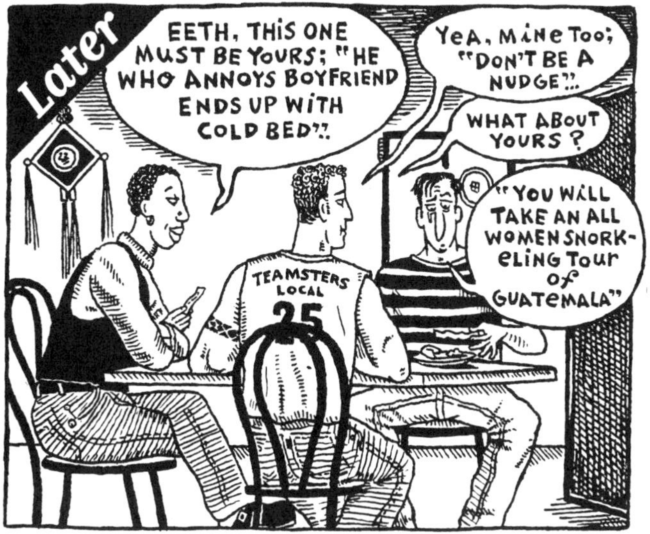
Later
EETH, THIS ONE MUST BE YOURS; "HE WHO ANNOYS BOYFRIEND ENDS UP WITH COLD BED".
YeA, MiNe Too; "DON'T BE A NUDGE".
WHAT ABOUT YOURS?
"YOU WiLL TAKE AN ALL WOMEN SNORK-ELiNG Tour of GUATEMALA"
TEAMSTERS LOCAL 25

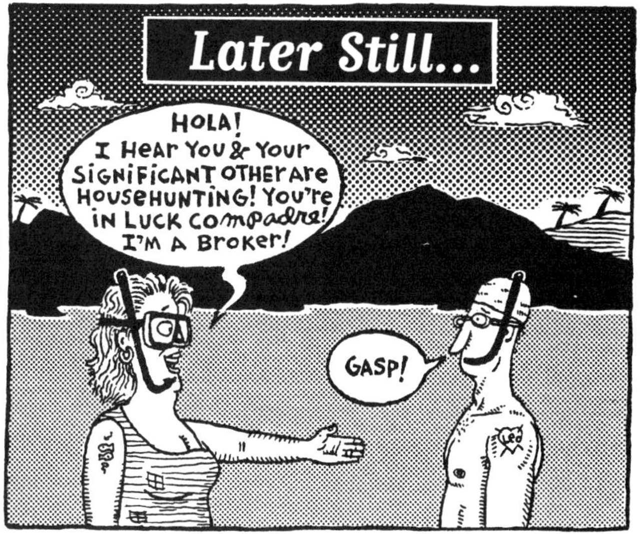
Later Still...
HOLA! I Hear You & Your SIGNiFICANT OTHEr are HOUSEHUNTING! You're in LUCK compadre! I'M A Broker!
GASP!

Getting to "oh, Yeah"...
Early one morning when the issue of moving in together wasn't on the agenda.
OH..
Oh..
OH...
DOUG..?
10 seconds to orgasm
...5..
...about BUYING a PLACE TOGETHER..
Yeah.. ..oh Yeah...
WELL, OK HONEY, IF YOU are SURE THAT'S WHAT YOU REALLY WANT..

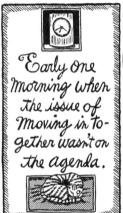

After the holding, the Cum toweling, & the Washing up.
So, I'M GONNA CALL The realtor NOW.
My Palpable ambivalence FAILING to DISSUADE YOU FROM THIS course of ACTION, Apparently...
apparently NOT...
ZELDA KLEIN GAY GHETTO REAL ESTATE MAVEN
Zelda, Dougie says He's Ready To buy...
FABULOUS I've GOT Several OPEN HOUSES & THINK YOU SHOULD See...
NOK NOK
OH DOUG, you'LL NEED PANTS..
INSIDE DOUG'S Head:

OK, We're STARTING OFF WITH SOMETHING THAT'S ProbabLY A BIT ROOMY TO SUIT~but IT'S IMPorTANT TO SHOW RANGE & CONTEXT..
and The NEIGHborHOOD! WELL IT'S REALLY "UP and coming"
and THIS PLACE is FABULOUS! - WAIT 'TILL you See THE ceiLINGS!
I'LL bet The poor FoLKS Forced TO Move OUT-THOUGHT SO ....
Oh CHARLOTTE, DON'T BE SUCH a SOUrPUSS..
SEE DOUGIE I TOLD YOU THIS WOULD BE FUN!
BUCKY AND CHARLOTTE, ALONG For MORAL SUPPORT
...BUT.... IT'S a... CATHEDRAL...
WELL yes,... BUT.. IT COMES WITH PARKING..
SWEETheart, KEEP AN OPEN MIND.. THE STAINED GLASS IS NICE...
WON'T THE ArCHBISHOP OBJECT?
She JUST bought A LOFT DOWNTOWN ...
Hey, are ALTar BOYS INCLUDED?

2 Ships Passing...
WESTON
With Ethan Green..
hey...
hey..
WHAT DO YOU LOOK LIKE?
BLAH BLAHBLAH
A MEETING ON THE PHONE LINES LEADS TO A MIDDLE OF THE NIGHT, IN-PERSON RENDEZVOUS AT A DOWNTOWN HOTEL..
NOK NOK
YIKES! ETHAN GREEN!
OH WOW.. JASON CHANG..
THIS IS A LITTLE EMBARRASSING
I'LL SAY..

SO... WHERE'S DOUG?
..KIND OF A LONG STORY. ..WHERE'S TIM & CARLOS..?
..NOT SURE I FEEL LIKE TALKING ABOUT IT.. ..Y'KNOW, YOU'RE KIND OF A GOSSIP..
DON'T TELL TODD ABOUT THIS.
OR ANYONE ELSE, I GUESS.
YEAH.
ONE ILLICIT HOUR LATER..
SO, REALLY, WHATS UP WITH YOU?
JEEZ, I DUNNO, JUST HORNEY & BOR-ED. DOUG'S OFF VISITING HIS PAR-ENTS AGAIN. HE HAD THIS NEAR NERVOUS BREAK DOWN AFTER OUR REALTOR DRAGGED US TO A DOZEN OPEN HOUSES LAST WEEKEND. -WE'RE THINK-ING OF BUYING A PLACE...

HOW ABOUT YOU? LAST I HEARD YOUR THREE-WAY UNION WAS PRETTY BLISSFULL...

IT USUALLY IS ~ EXCEPT FOR WHEN TIM'S, OR CARLOS'S FAMILY ARE VISITING. A MARRIAGE BETWEEN 2 MEN THEY CAN HANDLE ~ BETWEEN 3 MEN IS A LITTLE MORE "PROGRESSIVE" THAN ANYONE CAN STAND... SO... I'M KIND'A HOME-LESS UNTIL SUNDAY NITE WHEN THE BADILLOS ~ CARLOS'S PARENTS ~ RETURN TO SAN ANTONIO. WELL, NOT *homeless* EXACTLY ~ TIM PUT ME UP HERE AT THE WESTON ~ BUT I GOT PRETTY LONELY ~ SO I STARTED WORKING THE PHONES..

SO TIM'S PICKING UP THE TAB FOR ALL THIS?

YOU'RE **DAMN RIGHT** HE'S PAYING. HE'S LUCKY I WAS WILLING TO GO AT *all*!

..AND SO, ABANDONED BY THEIR SIGNIF-ICANT OTHERS, HOWEVER TEMPORARILY, THE GUYS CHOOSE THE ONLY OPTION LEFT AVAILABLE...

HELLO, ROOMSERVICE, WE'D LIKE A COU-PLE OF STEAKS, RARE, AND A NICE MERLOT, & CAV-IAR, OH, AND COCONUT LAYER CAKE.. AND OYSTERS.. ..AND

109

on the ~~air~~
ear
So Here you ARE, another DAY ON THE JOB as Personal ASSISTANT To TV WeATherman Monty Poole.
LAST Week AT A SENIOR CITIZEN'S EVENT
WELL HOW'r You YOUNG LADY?
DID YOU KNOW IT'S MY BirTH-DAY, I'M 87!
Mercy! I THOUGHT YOU Were SWEET 16... ETHAN, GIVE THIS LADY A HAND
Yes MONTY (yawn)
are YOU AL Reuker?
HI MONTY FAN
Actually, MONTY is OUT OF THE COUNTry ATTEND-ing A WEATHerman's CONVENTION IN BANGKOK..
Gary Greenway VANCOUVer TV WeATherman

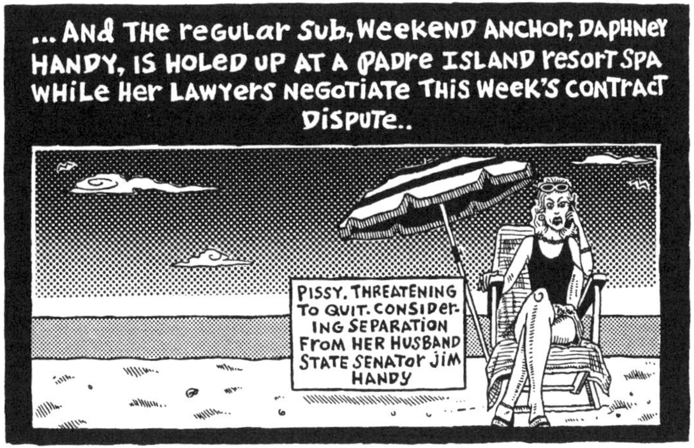
...AND THE REGULAR SUB, WEEKEND ANCHOR, DAPHNEY HANDY, IS HOLED UP AT A PADRE ISLAND RESORT SPA WHILE HER LAWYERS NEGOTIATE THIS WEEK'S CONTRACT DISPUTE..
PISSY. THREATENING TO QUIT. CONSIDERING SEPARATION FROM HER HUSBAND STATE SENATOR JIM HANDY

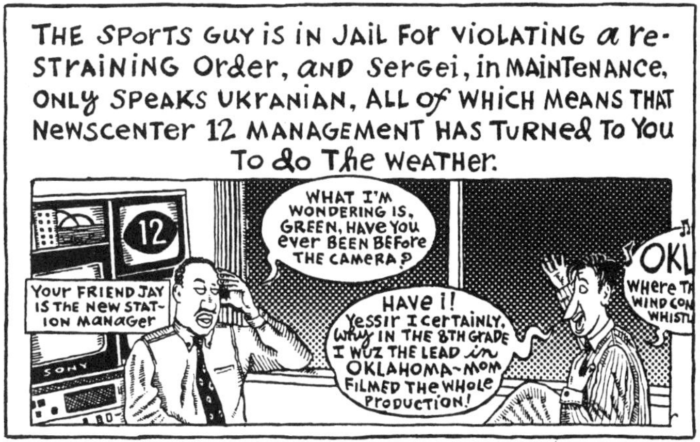
THE SPORTS GUY IS IN JAIL FOR VIOLATING A RESTRAINING ORDER, AND SERGEI, IN MAINTENANCE, ONLY SPEAKS UKRANIAN, ALL OF WHICH MEANS THAT NEWSCENTER 12 MANAGEMENT HAS TURNED TO YOU TO DO THE WEATHER.
12
WHAT I'M WONDERING IS, GREEN, HAVE YOU EVER BEEN BEFORE THE CAMERA?
YOUR FRIEND JAY IS THE NEW STATION MANAGER
HAVE I! YESSIR I CERTAINLY, WHY IN THE 8TH GRADE I WUZ THE LEAD IN OKLAHOMA~MOM FILMED THE WHOLE PRODUCTION!
SONY

This is big news in the ghetto, where your friends throw a little party to tape your 15 minutes..
NOW NEWS 12
MRS. GREEN

And since you are being critiqued by every queen in the city, mysterious forces of the cosmos conspire to make you look unattractive. Despite the best efforts of Michael, Channel 12's stylist, you've apparently grown a hair out of the top of your ear...
15 seconds 'till air...
Hey check out the new guy-ear hair..
Seen it.
GASP
OMYGOD

Hats Off To the Hat Sisters

At the Hat Sisters Anniversary Party, Number One, which is the name of one of the Sisters told assembled guests how much he loves Number Two, which is the name of the other..

Exactly which anniversary this was, wasn't specified.. Despite your efforts at clarification.

Well, I mean, which one is this?.. How long have you been together?

Since before you were born..

Since before Dolly Madison was born..

We aren't saying, so quit being fresh...

113

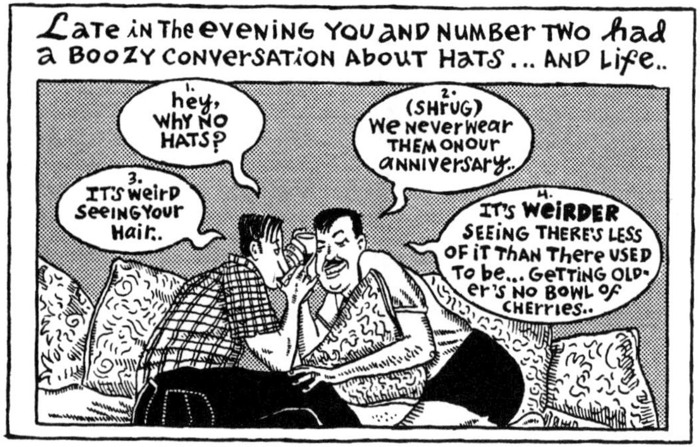
Late in The evening you and number two had a boozy conversation about hats... and life..
1. hey, why no hats?
2. (shrug) We never wear them on our anniversary..
3. It's weird seeing your hair..
4. It's WEIRDER seeing there's less of it than there used to be... getting older's no bowl of cherries..

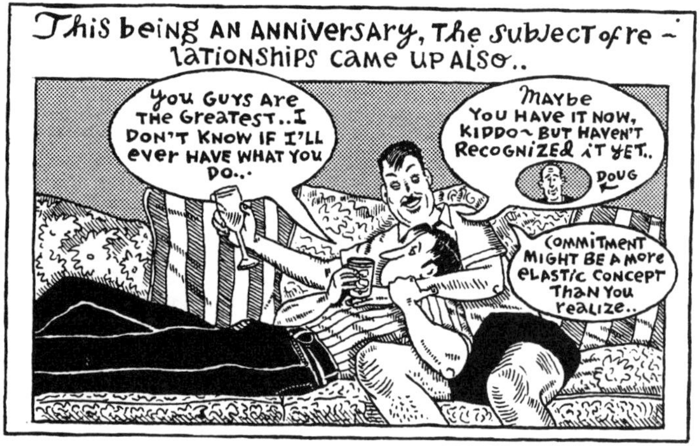
This being an anniversary, The subject of relationships came up also..
You guys are the greatest..I don't know if I'll ever have what you do...
Maybe you have it now, kiddo~ but haven't recognized it yet..
DOUG
Commitment might be a more elastic concept than you realize..

Not that you were all that receptive to what the old girl had to say..

OH GOD, LET'S NOT DISCUSS "OPEN RELATIONSHIPS" again...

OK SUGAR, WHAT **SHALL** WE DISCUSS ? SPORTS ? ROTH IRA's ? THAT HAIRDO ON LINDA TRIPP ?

Later, Number One passed out—she said the fumes from whatever Bucky was smoking made her dizzy...

THE SMELL IS REMINDING HIM OF A SYLVESTER CONCERT HE ONCE ATTENDED.

Number Two, very much awake, arm-twisted you all into crossing the street & dancing at "Club Rubio," an ongoing house party at the residence of these two sweet blond friends of Tim's & Carlos's...

115

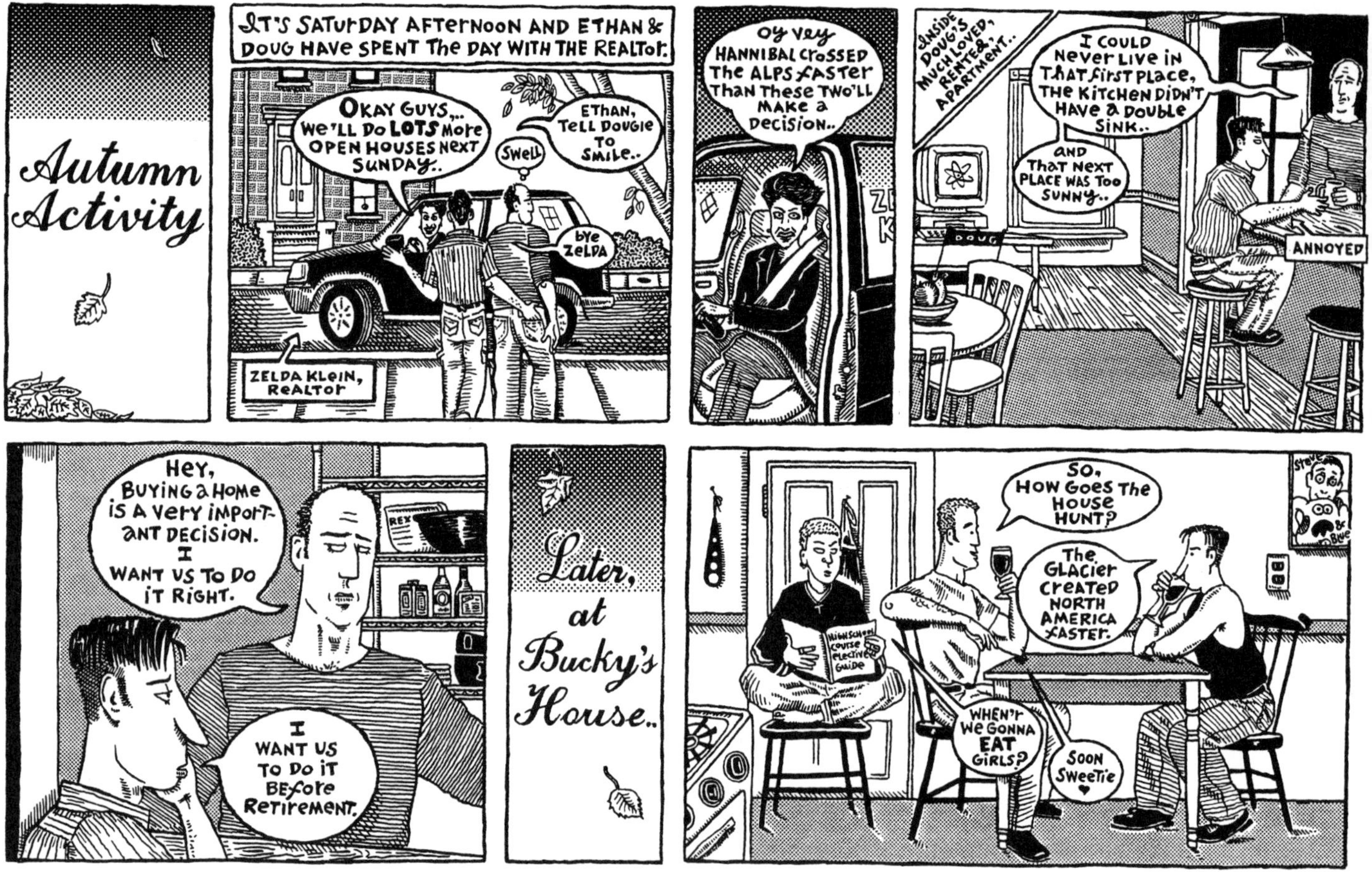
Autumn Activity
It's Saturday afternoon and Ethan & Doug have spent the day with the realtor.
Okay guys,.. We'll do LOTS more open houses next Sunday..
Swell
Ethan, tell Dougie to smile..
bye Zelda
Zelda Klein, Realtor
Oy vey Hannibal crossed the Alps faster than these two'll make a decision..
Inside Doug's much loved, rented, apartment..
I could never live in that first place, the kitchen didn't have a double sink..
and that next place was too sunny..
ANNOYED
DOUG
Hey, buying a home is a very important decision. I want us to do it right.
I want us to do it before retirement.
Later, at Bucky's House..
So, how goes the house hunt?
The glacier created North America faster.
High School Course Elective Guide
When're we gonna eat girls?
Soon sweetie ♥

HE LOVES YOU.. HE JUST ALSO LOVES HAVING HIS OWN PLACE. THINGS COULD BE WORSE.
HOW?
WELL.. HE COULD NOT LOVE YOU, AND LOVE HAVING HIS OWN PLACE
.. OR HE COULD NOT LOVE YOU but LOVE YOUR PLACE.. OR MAYBE
OK ok.. THANK YOU VERY MUCH..
Meanwhile, Sinister Plans are afoot á Montréal..
CALL ETHAN, AND TELL him YOU'VE FINALLY DECIDED TO TAKE HIM UP ON THAT KIND OFFER TO PUT YOU UP..
RIGHT.
ETHAN'S "EX," ETIENNE
HIS GALPAL LEEZA

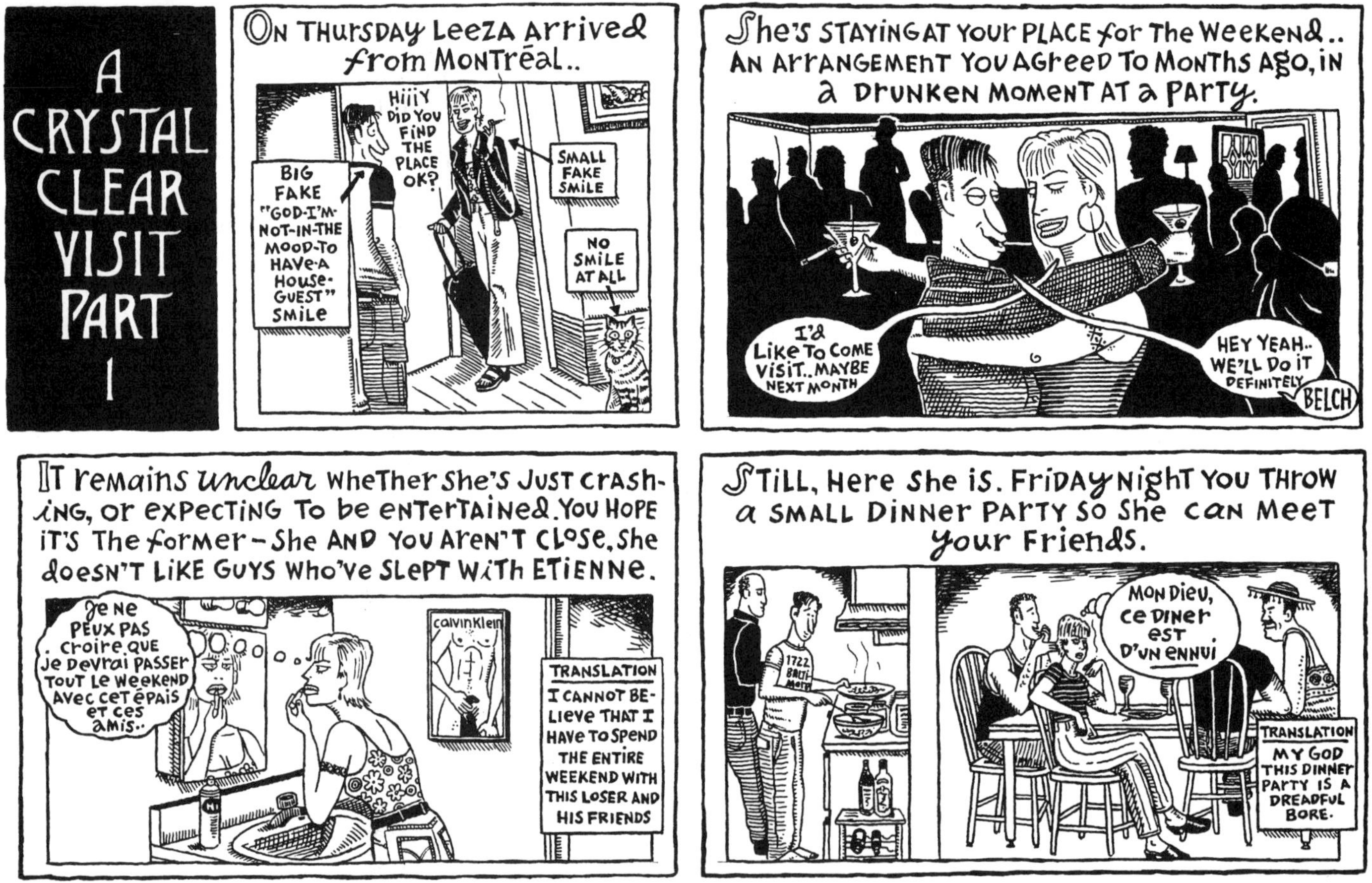
A CRYSTAL CLEAR VISIT PART 1
On Thursday Leeza arrived from Montréal..
Hiiiy did you find the place ok?
BIG FAKE "GOD-I'M-NOT-IN-THE-MOOD-TO-HAVE-A-HOUSE-GUEST" SMILE
SMALL FAKE SMILE
NO SMILE AT ALL
She's staying at your place for the weekend.. An arrangement you agreed to months ago, in a drunken moment at a party.
I'd like to come visit.. maybe next month
Hey yeah.. we'll do it definitely
BELCH
It remains unclear whether she's just crashing, or expecting to be entertained. You hope it's the former – she and you aren't close, she doesn't like guys who've slept with Etienne.
Je ne peux pas croire que je devrai passer tout le weekend avec cet épais et ces amis..
calvinklein
TRANSLATION
I CANNOT BELIEVE THAT I HAVE TO SPEND THE ENTIRE WEEKEND WITH THIS LOSER AND HIS FRIENDS
Still, here she is. Friday night you throw a small dinner party so she can meet your friends.
Mon Dieu, ce diner est d'un ennui
TRANSLATION
MY GOD THIS DINNER PARTY IS A DREADFUL BORE.

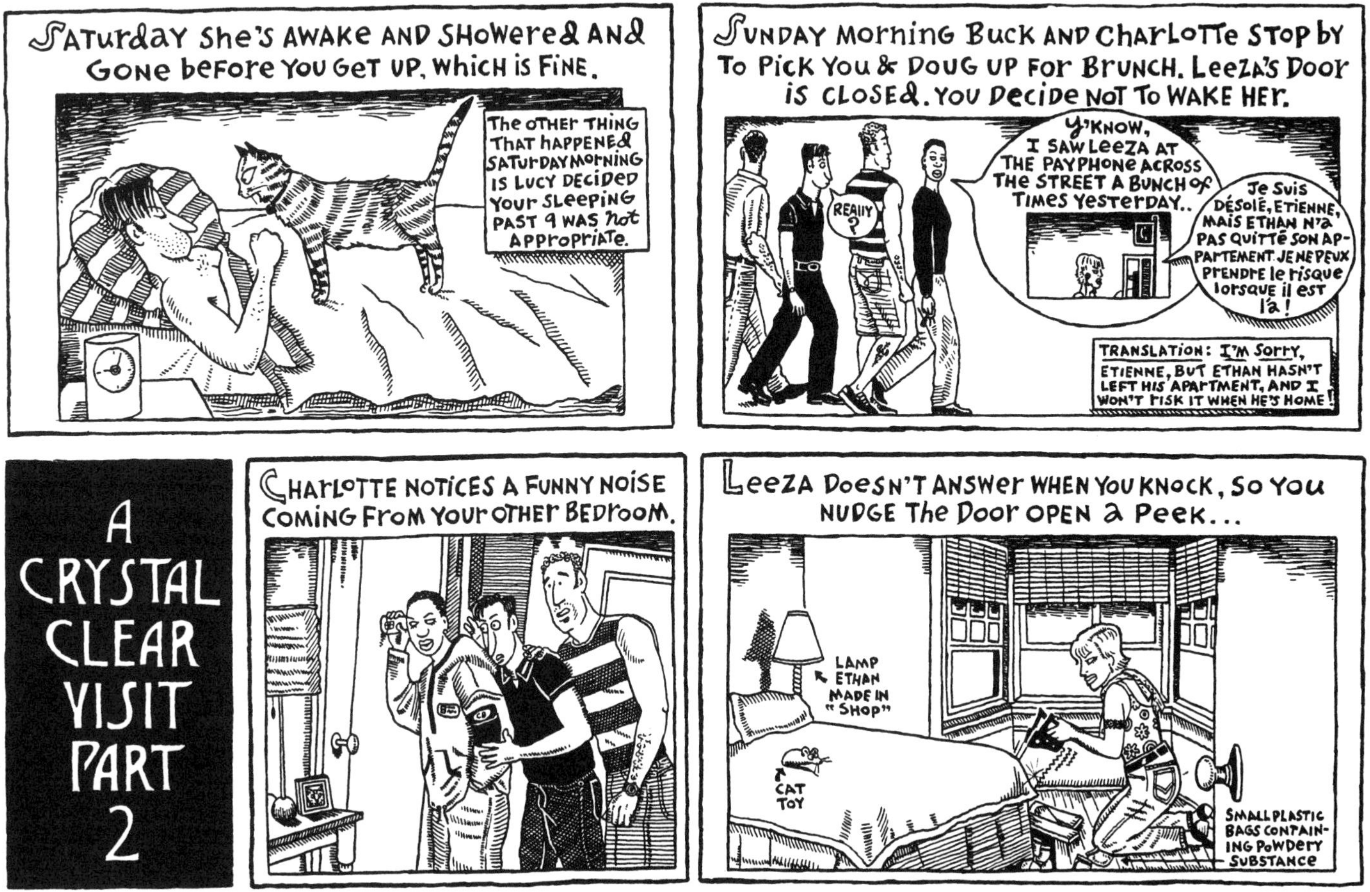
SATURDAY SHE'S AWAKE AND SHOWERED AND GONE BEFORE YOU GET UP, WHICH IS FINE.
THE OTHER THING THAT HAPPENED SATURDAY MORNING IS LUCY DECIDED YOUR SLEEPING PAST 9 WAS *NOT* APPROPRIATE.
SUNDAY MORNING BUCK AND CHARLOTTE STOP BY TO PICK YOU & DOUG UP FOR BRUNCH. LEEZA'S DOOR IS CLOSED. YOU DECIDE NOT TO WAKE HER.
Y'KNOW, I SAW LEEZA AT THE PAYPHONE ACROSS THE STREET A BUNCH OF TIMES YESTERDAY..
REALLY?
JE SUIS DÉSOLÉ, ETIENNE, MAIS ETHAN N'A PAS QUITTÉ SON APPARTEMENT. JE NE PEUX PRENDRE LE RISQUE LORSQUE IL EST LÀ!
TRANSLATION: I'M SORRY, ETIENNE, BUT ETHAN HASN'T LEFT HIS APARTMENT, AND I WON'T RISK IT WHEN HE'S HOME!
A CRYSTAL CLEAR VISIT PART 2
CHARLOTTE NOTICES A FUNNY NOISE COMING FROM YOUR OTHER BEDROOM.
LEEZA DOESN'T ANSWER WHEN YOU KNOCK, SO YOU NUDGE THE DOOR OPEN A PEEK...
LAMP ETHAN MADE IN "SHOP"
CAT TOY
SMALL PLASTIC BAGS CONTAINING POWDERY SUBSTANCE

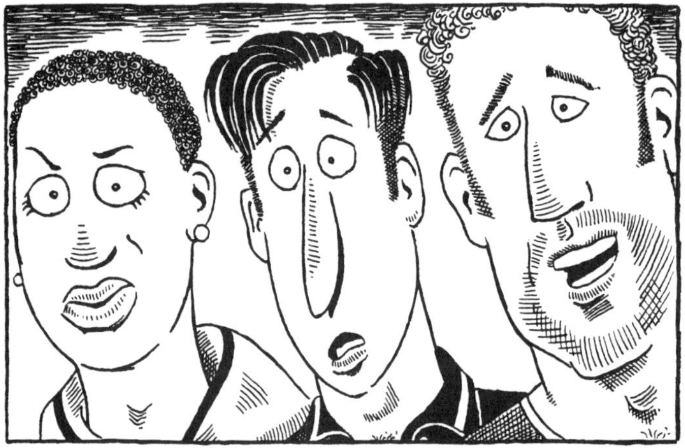

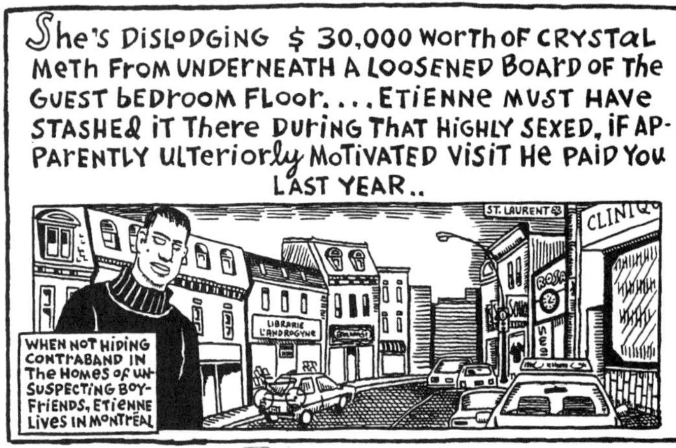

She's DISLODGING $ 30,000 WORTH OF CRYSTAL METH FROM UNDERNEATH A LOOSENED BOARD OF THE GUEST BEDROOM FLOOR. . . . ETIENNE MUST HAVE STASHED IT THERE DURING THAT HIGHLY SEXED, IF APPARENTLY ULTERIORLY MOTIVATED VISIT HE PAID YOU LAST YEAR..
ST. LAURENT
CLINIQ
LIBRARIE L'ANDROGYNE
WHEN NOT HIDING CONTRABAND IN THE HOMES OF UNSUSPECTING BOYFRIENDS, ETIENNE LIVES IN MONTRÉAL

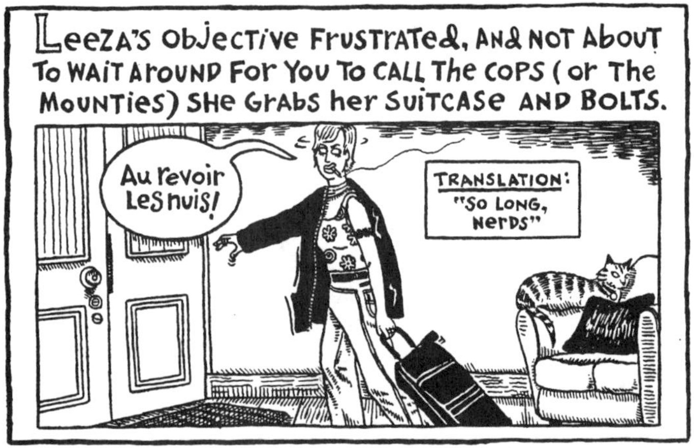

LEEZA'S OBJECTIVE FRUSTRATED, AND NOT ABOUT TO WAIT AROUND FOR YOU TO CALL THE COPS (OR THE MOUNTIES) SHE GRABS HER SUITCASE AND BOLTS.
Au revoir Les nuis!
TRANSLATION: "SO LONG, NERDS"

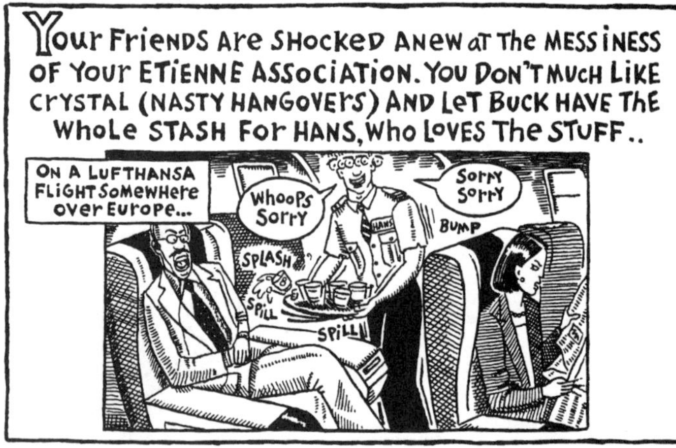

YOUR FRIENDS ARE SHOCKED ANEW AT THE MESSINESS OF YOUR ETIENNE ASSOCIATION. YOU DON'T MUCH LIKE CRYSTAL (NASTY HANGOVERS) AND LET BUCK HAVE THE WHOLE STASH FOR HANS, WHO LOVES THE STUFF..
ON A LUFTHANSA FLIGHT SOMEWHERE OVER EUROPE...
Whoops Sorry
Sorry Sorry
HANS
BUMP
SPLASH
SPILL
SPILL

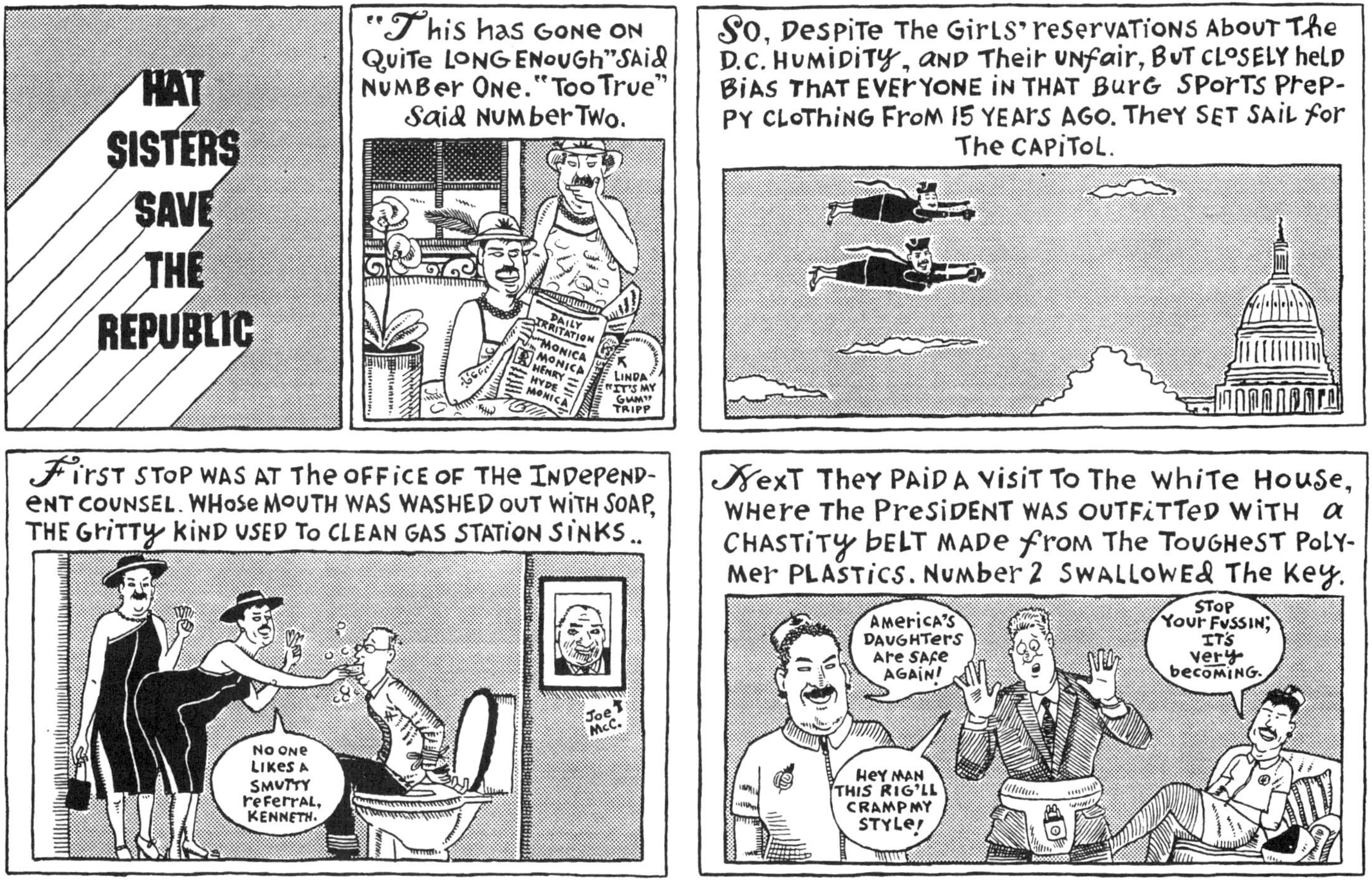
HAT SISTERS SAVE THE REPUBLIC
"This has gone on quite long enough" said Number One. "Too true" said Number Two.
DAILY IRRITATION
"MONICA MONICA HENRY HYDE MONICA
LINDA "IT'S MY GUM" TRIPP
So, despite the girls' reservations about the D.C. humidity, and their unfair, but closely held bias that everyone in that burg sports preppy clothing from 15 years ago. They set sail for the Capitol.
First stop was at the office of the Independent Counsel. Whose mouth was washed out with soap, the gritty kind used to clean gas station sinks..
No one likes a smutty referral, Kenneth.
Joe McC.
Next they paid a visit to the White House, where the President was outfitted with a chastity belt made from the toughest polymer plastics. Number 2 swallowed the key.
America's daughters are safe again!
Hey man this rig'll cramp my style!
Stop your fussin; it's very becoming.

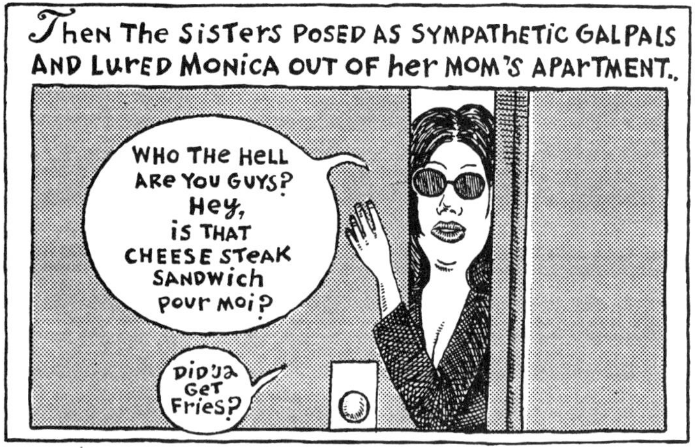
Then The SisTers POSED AS SYMPATHETIC GALPALS AND LureD MONICA OUT OF her MOM'S APARTMENT..
WHO THE HELL ARE YOU GUYS? Hey, is THAT CHEESE STeak SANDWich pour moi?
DiD'ja GeT Fries?

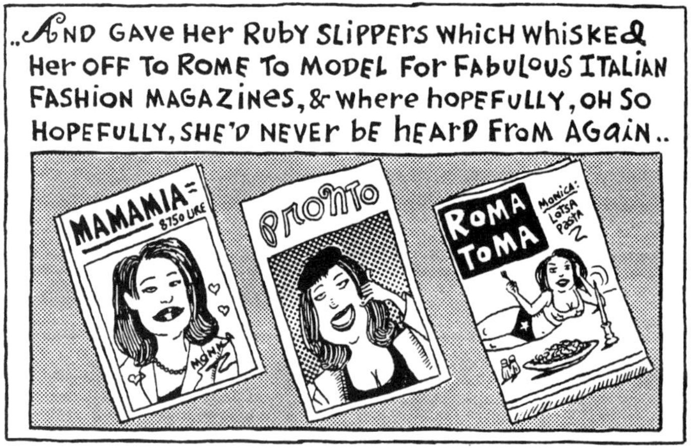
..AND GAVE Her Ruby SLIPPERS WHICH WHISKED Her OFF TO ROME TO MODEL For FABULOUS ITALIAN FASHION MAGAZINES, & Where hopeFULLY, OH SO HOPEFULLY, SHE'D NEVER bE heArD From AGain..
MAMAMIA
8750 LIRE
PRONTO
ROMA TOMA
MONICA: LOTSA PASTA

The Thing About Your Office's Holiday Party With Ethan Green
You're introduced to the mutants, ex-cons and misfits paired up with your colleagues in private life...
HEY! uh... EVAN!.. HEY, I'd LIKE YOU TO MEET MY LADY, SQUEEKY. SHE USED TO BE WITH THE MANSON FAMILY!
YIKES
CHANNEL 12
The boss metamorphs into a human being for a couple of hours, Making everyone uncomfortable...
OH SURE, I KNOW THIS PERSONA I'VE DEVELOPED, MONTY POOLE TV WEATHER MAVEN IS A BIT RIDICULOUS... IT WASN'T SUPPOSED TO TURN OUT THIS WAY..... I STARTED AS A SHAKESPEAREAN ACTOR,.. DID SUMMERSTOCK, A BBC SPECIAL... BUT I WAS BROKE, & THIS RADIO STATION IN FT. WAYNE NEEDED AN ANNOUNCER...
OH GOD WE'RE BONDING

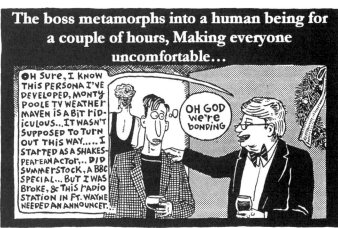

Previously undetected office romances solar flare into visibility…

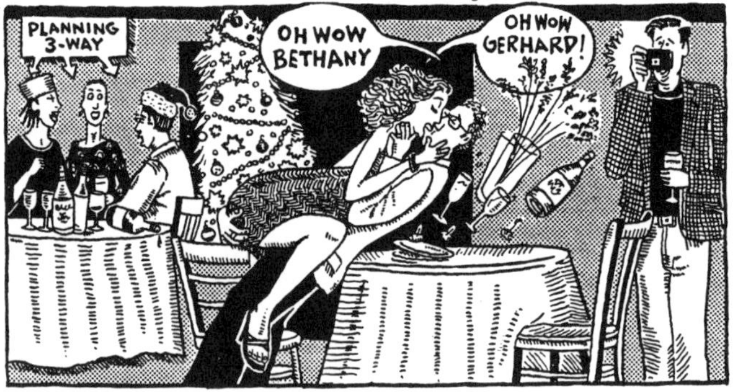
PLANNING 3-WAY
OH WOW BETHANY
OH WOW GERHARD!

Certain co-workers release their inner-child, expressing themselves in festive holiday sweaters…

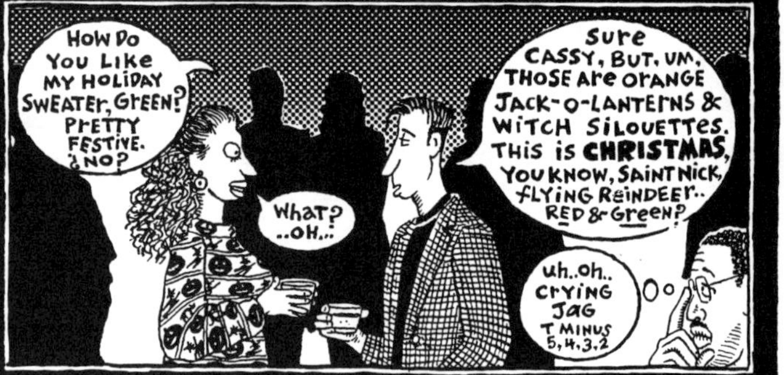
HOW DO YOU LIKE MY HOLIDAY SWEATER, GREEN? PRETTY FESTIVE. ¿NO?
WHAT? ..OH..
SURE CASSY, BUT, UM, THOSE ARE ORANGE JACK-O-LANTERNS & WITCH SILOUETTES. THIS IS CHRISTMAS, YOU KNOW, SAINT NICK, FLYING REINDEER.. RED & GREEN?
UH..OH.. CRYING JAG T MINUS 5,4,3,2

The free flow of alcohol loosens tongues…

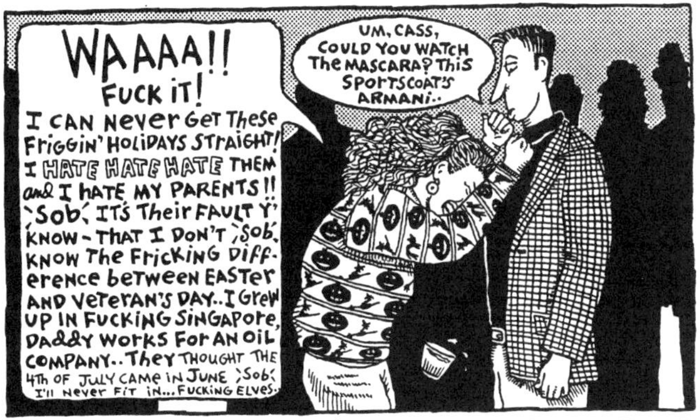

WAAAA!! FUCK IT! I CAN NEVER GET THESE FRIGGIN' HOLIDAYS STRAIGHT! I HATE HATE HATE THEM and I HATE MY PARENTS!! SOB IT'S THEIR FAULT Y' KNOW – THAT I DON'T SOB KNOW THE FRICKING DIFFERENCE BETWEEN EASTER AND VETERAN'S DAY.. I GREW UP IN FUCKING SINGAPORE, DADDY WORKS FOR AN OIL COMPANY.. THEY THOUGHT THE 4TH OF JULY CAME IN JUNE SOB I'LL NEVER FIT IN... FUCKING ELVES.
UM, CASS, COULD YOU WATCH THE MASCARA? THIS SPORTSCOAT'S ARMANI..

You get your annual opportunity to come-on to the kid who works for the company that takes care of the office's plants…

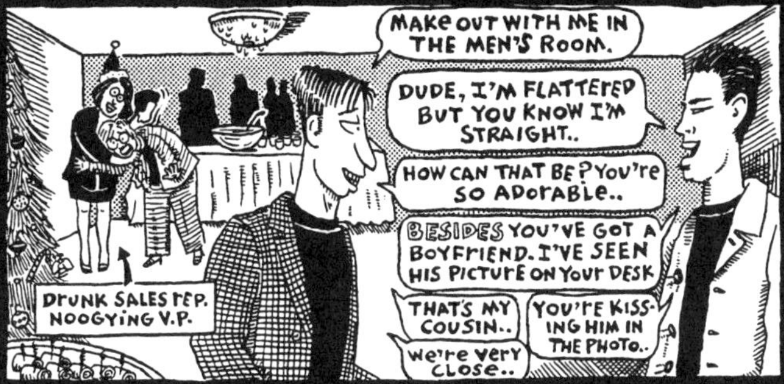

MAKE OUT WITH ME IN THE MEN'S ROOM.
DUDE, I'M FLATTERED BUT YOU KNOW I'M STRAIGHT..
HOW CAN THAT BE? YOU'RE SO ADORABLE..
BESIDES YOU'VE GOT A BOYFRIEND. I'VE SEEN HIS PICTURE ON YOUR DESK
THAT'S MY COUSIN..
WE'RE VERY CLOSE..
YOU'RE KISSING HIM IN THE PHOTO..
DRUNK SALES REP. NOOGYING V.P.

millennium

bugs

With ethan green

Y2k
Hysteria
Has hit
Ethan Green's
Place of
Employment
Newschannel 12

Our COMPUTERS WILL CRASH! OUR Air TRAFFIC CONTROL WILL FAIL! GRANDMA'S SOCIAL SECURITY CHECK WILL GET LOST!..The "Furby" i GOT For CHRISTMAS WILL ONLY SPEAK GIBBERISH!
EETH'S CAMERA-MAN PAL RODNEY
"FURBYS" ARE SUPPOSED TO ONLY SPEAK GIBBERISH..
OH... Really? huh.. ...HEY, Wha'd YOU GET for XMAS?..
"BILLY'S GRIZZLY BEAR-UNCLE DON"
DAMN. I WANTED ONE OF THOSE..
DON DON
GROWL

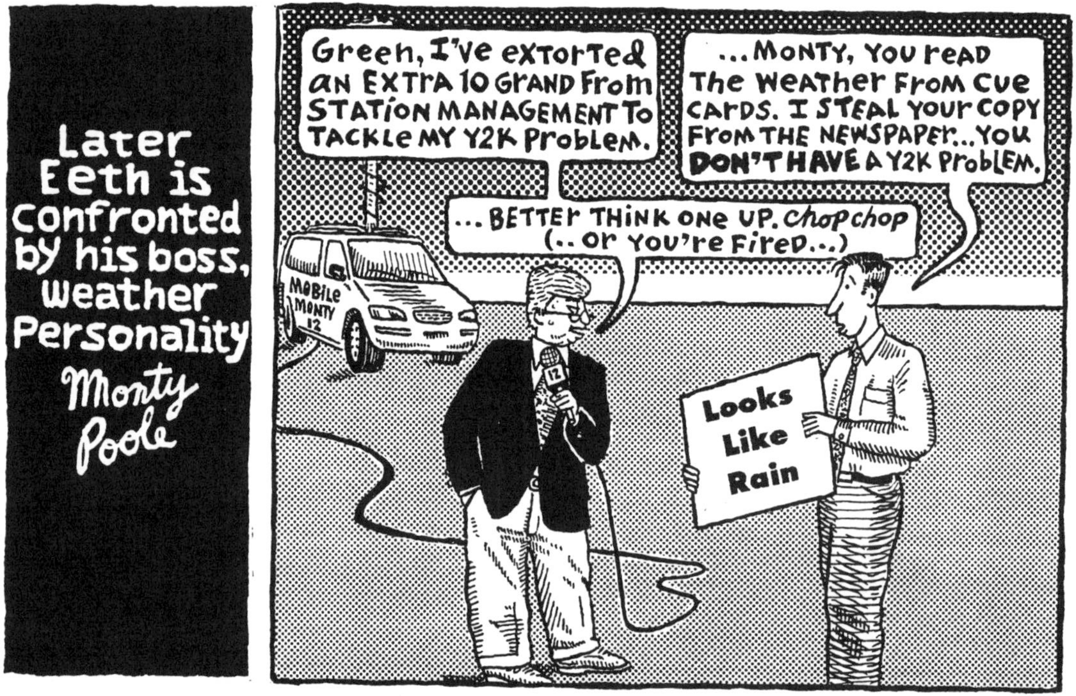
Later Eeth is confronted by his boss, weather Personality Monty Poole
Green, I've extorted an EXTRA 10 GRAND From STATION MANAGEMENT To TACKLE MY Y2K Problem.
... BETTER THINK ONE UP. chop chop (.. or You're Fired...)
... MONTY, YOU READ The Weather From Cue Cards. I STEAL Your COPY From THE NEWSPAPER... YOU DON'T HAVE A Y2K Problem.
MOBILE MONTY 12
Looks Like Rain

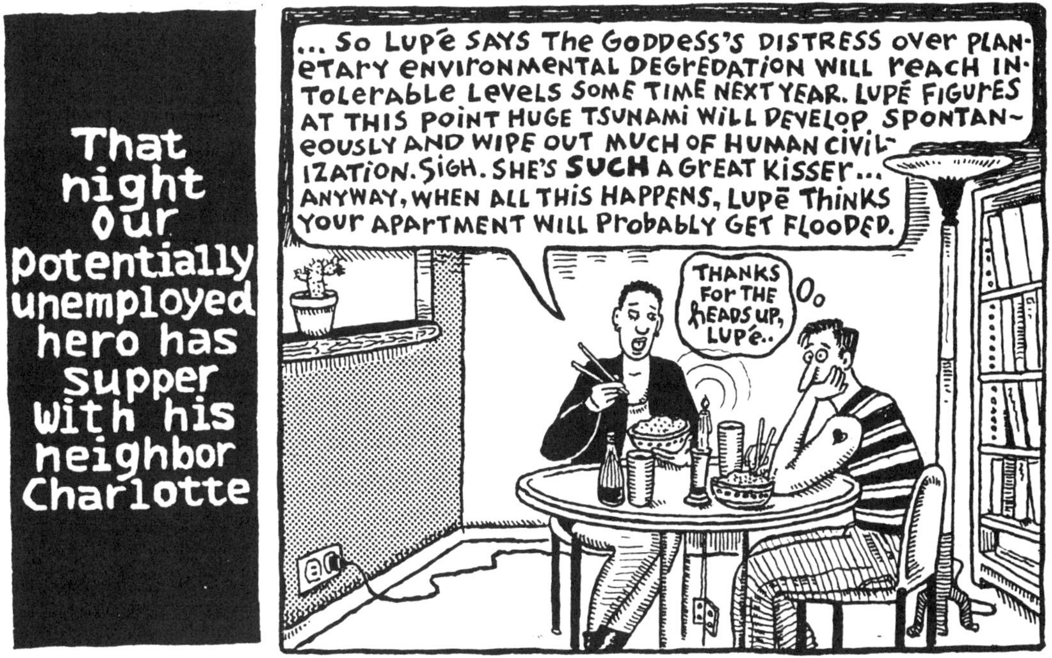
That night our potentially unemployed hero has supper with his neighbor Charlotte
... So Lupé says The Goddess's distress over planetary environmental degredation will reach intolerable levels some time next year. Lupé figures at this point huge tsunami will develop spontaneously and wipe out much of human civilization. Sigh. She's SUCH a great kisser... Anyway, when all this happens, Lupē thinks your apartment will probably get flooded.
Thanks for the heads up, Lupé..

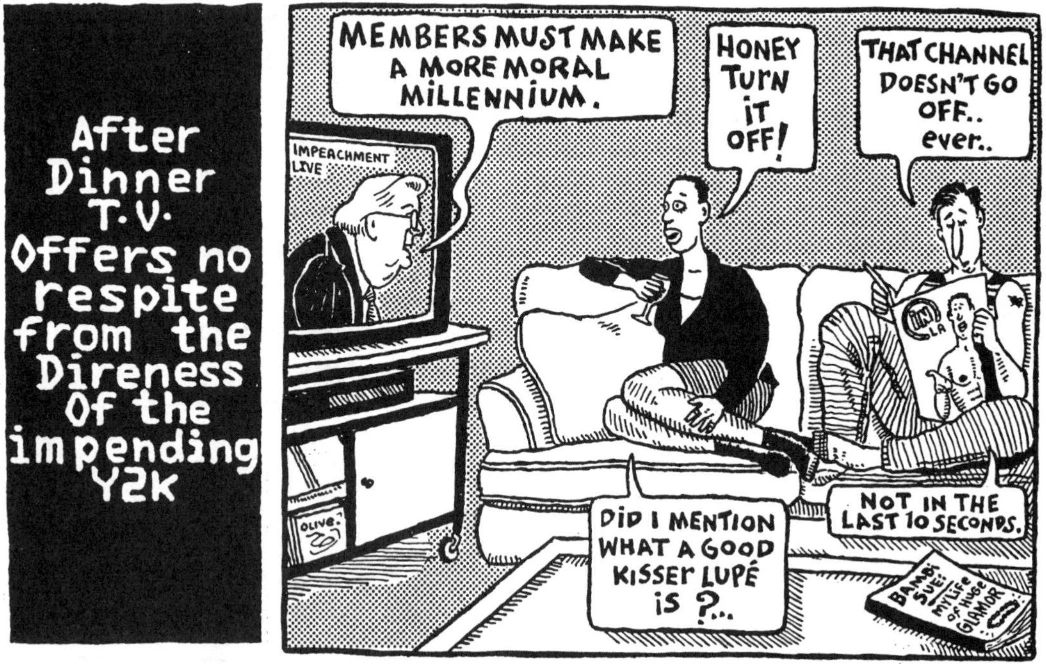
After Dinner T.V. Offers no respite from the Direness Of the impending Y2K
IMPEACHMENT LIVE
MEMBERS MUST MAKE A MORE MORAL MILLENNIUM.
HONEY TURN IT OFF!
THAT CHANNEL DOESN'T GO OFF.. ever..
DID I MENTION WHAT A GOOD KISSER LUPÉ IS ?...
NOT IN THE LAST 10 SECONDS.
OLIVE
BAMBI SUE: MY LIFE OF HUGE GLAMOR

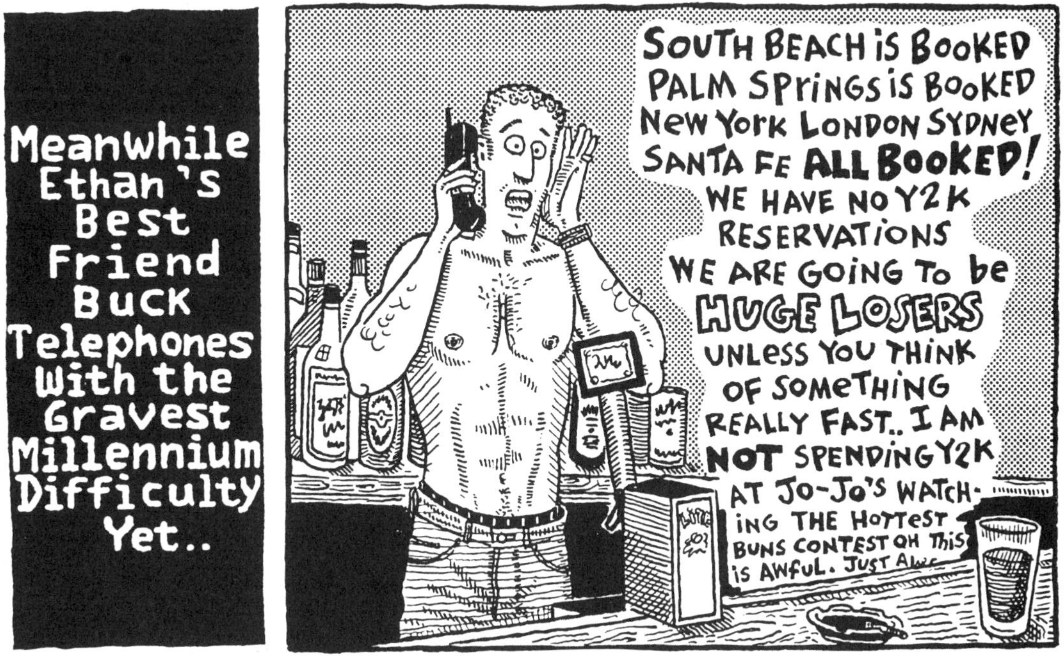
Meanwhile Ethan's Best Friend Buck Telephones With the Gravest Millennium Difficulty Yet..
SOUTH BEACH IS BOOKED PALM SPRINGS IS BOOKED NEW YORK LONDON SYDNEY SANTA FE ALL BOOKED! WE HAVE NO Y2K RESERVATIONS WE ARE GOING TO BE HUGE LOSERS UNLESS YOU THINK OF SOMETHING REALLY FAST.. I AM NOT SPENDING Y2K AT JO-JO'S WATCHING THE HOTTEST BUNS CONTEST OH THIS IS AWFUL. JUST

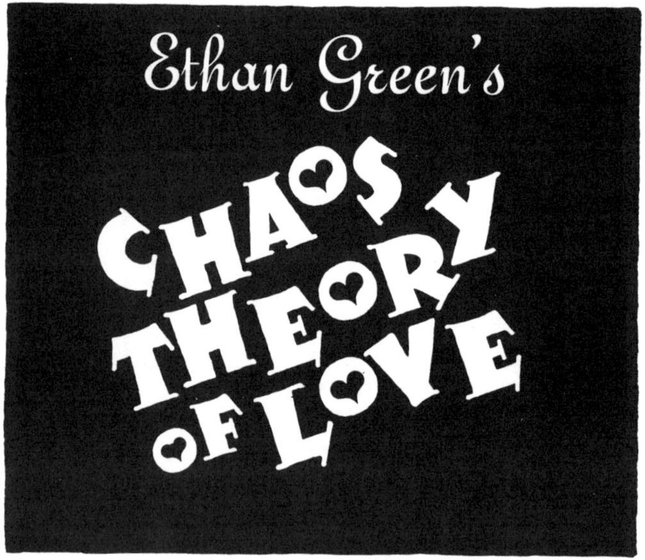
Ethan Green's
CHAOS THEORY OF LOVE

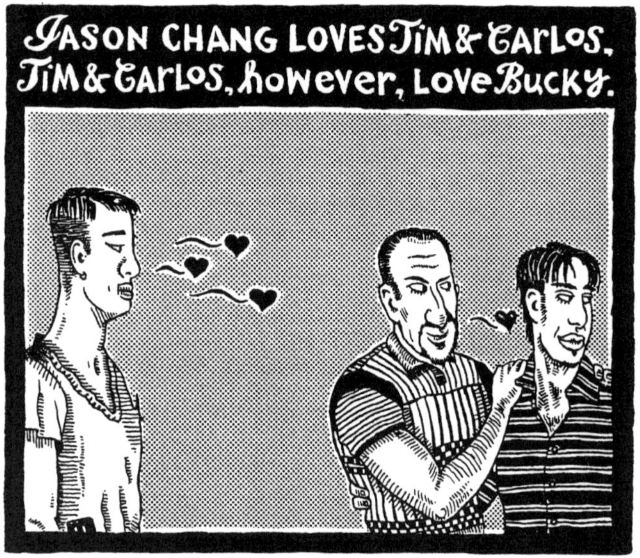
JASON CHANG LOVES TIM & CARLOS.
TIM & CARLOS, however, Love BUCKY.

BUCKY ONLY LOVES **HANS,** **HANS,** THOUGH, LOVES **LAST NIGHT'S TRICK.**

LAST NIGHT'S TRICK, *as it happens,* **REALLY LOVES LEEZA...**

BUT LEEZA, AS IS WELL DOCUMENTED, ONLY LOVES ETIENNE...

133

ETIENNE MOSTLY JUST LOVES ETIENNE, BUT OCCASIONALLY CAN BE FOUND TO LOVE CARLOS'S BEST GIRLFRIEND JAMES.

BUT CARLOS'S BEST GIRLFRIEND JAMES APPARENTLY LOVES ETHAN'S EX-LOVER, LEO.

LEO, SEVERAL YEARS TARDY, THINKS HE JUST MIGHT BE READY TO LOVE ETHAN.

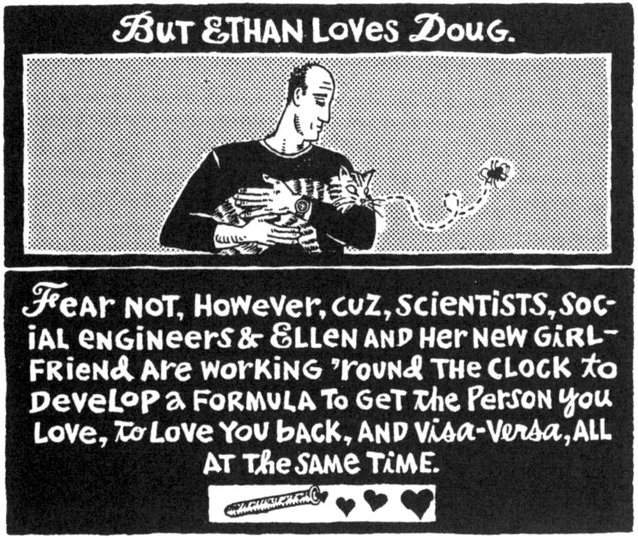
BUT ETHAN LOVES DOUG.
FEAR NOT, HOWEVER, CUZ, SCIENTISTS, SOCIAL ENGINEERS & ELLEN AND HER NEW GIRLFRIEND ARE WORKING 'ROUND THE CLOCK TO DEVELOP A FORMULA TO GET THE PERSON YOU LOVE, TO LOVE YOU BACK, AND VISA-VERSA, ALL AT THE SAME TIME.

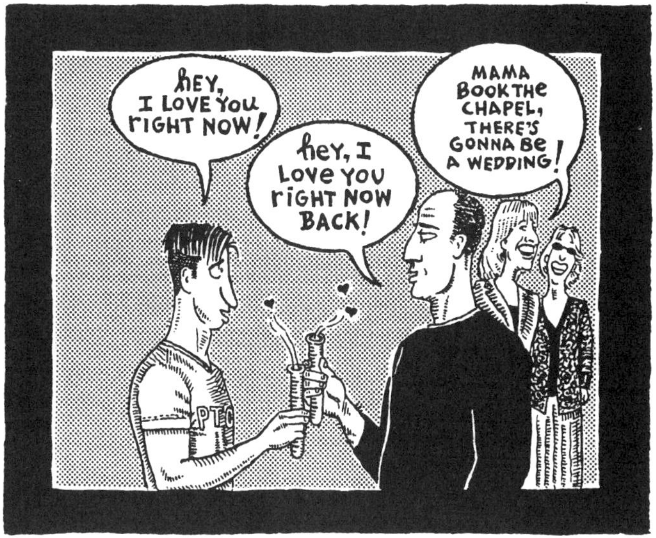
HEY, I LOVE YOU RIGHT NOW!
HEY, I LOVE YOU RIGHT NOW BACK!
MAMA BOOK THE CHAPEL, THERE'S GONNA BE A WEDDING!
PTC

*E*RIC ORNER sold his first cartoon to the *Chicago Daily News* in 1977 and has been drawing for publications ever since. Upon graduation from college, he worked as the editorial cartoonist for the *Concord Daily Monitor* in New Hampshire. His cartoons and illustrations have appeared in newspapers and magazines across the country, including the *Washington Post* and the *New Republic*. Eric's *Ethan Green* comic strip is published in weekly newspapers across the United States, Canada, and Britain.

Photograph by Stella Johnson